Partnerships for Inclusive Education

Participation is essential for inclusive education. But why is this and what does this mean? How can it be brought about?

Participation in the sense of *real* collaborative working has largely been elusive in any widespread sense. Increased partnership between professionals, particularly through the integration of services, heralds a major opportunity for child and parent participation, but one that seems in danger of being side-stepped. Drawing on substantial research evidence, this book looks at reasons for this situation, what is happening now, what developments and initiatives have been tried and what we can do to develop a culture of participation.

Some of the main threats to participation are discussed throughout this text:

- Has 'partnership' ever existed?
- Who is excluded from partnership?
- Which discourses have made participation elusive, and what are the implications – theoretical and practical – for how we move forward?

Liz Todd presents original ideas to both practitioners and academics to open up the complex processes that can frustrate participative practice. The PPC (Practice–People–Context) Model of collaborative inclusive practice helpfully guides people working with children and families in schools and services towards the development of a culture of participation. In combining socio-cultural ideas with post-structural thinking, the strong yet accessible theoretical basis to this book makes the ideas relevant to both an academic and an educational professional audience.

Liz Todd is senior lecturer and Director of Educational Psychology at the University of Newcastle upon Tyne, UK.

Partnerships for Inclusive Education

A critical approach to collaborative working

Liz Todd

160801

Routledge
Taylor & Francis Group

LONDON AND NEW YORK

First published 2007 by RoutledgeFalmer
2 Park Square, Milton Park, Abingdon, Oxon OX14 4RN

Simultaneously published in the USA and Canada
by RoutledgeFalmer
270 Madison Ave, New York, NY 10016

*RoutledgeFalmer is an imprint of the Taylor & Francis Group,
an informa business*

© 2007 Liz Todd

Typeset in Sabon by
RefineCatch Limited, Bungay, Suffolk
Printed and bound in Great Britain by
MPG Books Ltd, Bodmin, Cornwall

British Library Cataloguing in Publication Data
A catalogue record for this book is available from the British Library

Library of Congress Cataloging in Publication Data
A catalog record for this book has been requested

ISBN10: 0–415–29844–X (hbk)
ISBN10: 0–415–29845–8 (pbk)
ISBN10: 0–203–96749–6 (ebk)

ISBN13: 978–0–415–29844–5 (hbk)
ISBN13: 978–0–415–29845–2 (pbk)
ISBN13: 978–0–203–96749–2 (ebk)

Contents

Illustrations

Tables

Figures

Acknowledgements

Writing this book has been a journey – and one impossible without so many friends and colleagues discussing ideas and making comments on drafts. It would have been abandoned without the great support of Andy, Robin and Jake and the time they gave me to write. Final thanks to the people – children and adults – I have worked with in grappling myself with how to have real participation in schools and services, and from whom I have learnt so much.

1 What partnerships for what kind of inclusive education?

Introduction

Inclusive education is built – in schools and in local authorities – in many ways. New bricks are added to replace the old. Some forgotten friends are remembered and added with new cement. What makes the 'inclusion' wall secure, stops cracks developing, or stops it from leaning in directions where it could topple is partnership. Real partnership. Participation based on mutuality and respect. This book takes as its starting point the assumption that this crucial element of what makes inclusion robust is often absent, given lip-service, badly done or wrongly assumed. Partnership and participation are explored through what we know about what is currently happening, what we know about what makes them difficult to secure and ideas for practice. This chapter explains the key understandings that inform the book – some of them theoretical – and explains the structure of the book. It makes a case for the particular partnerships that are to be considered and explores what is meant by inclusive education.

There are probably countless ways to write a book on partnerships for inclusive education. I have chosen three areas that seem to speak very loudly for attention: these are areas where there have been substantial improvements but at the same time where there are real needs for change and improvement. They are all arenas for collaborative working that seem to be central to inclusion. These areas are: the participation of children and young people in schools and services; the partnership of parents with schools and with practitioners who work in services external to schools; and collaborative working between professionals and agencies. These three areas of collaboration are epitomised in the following quotes from research and policy, which illustrate their importance for different kinds of inclusive education, and introduce some of the issues and tensions.

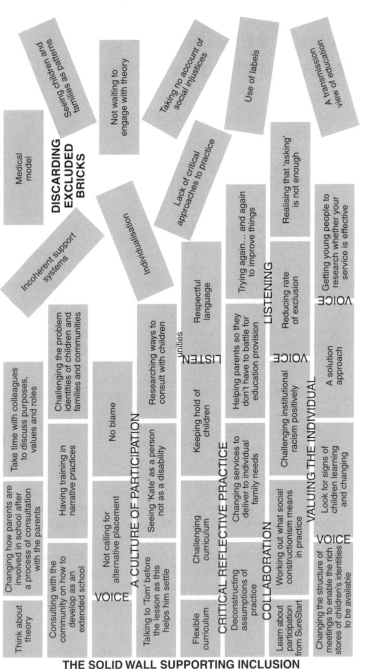

Figure 1.1 Inclusions and exclusions: building a solid foundation.

DISCARDING EXCLUDED BRICKS

Seeing children and families as patterns

Not waiting to engage with theory

Taking no account of social injustices

Use of labels

A transmission view of education

Medical model

Lack of critical approaches to practice

Incoherent support systems

Individualisation

Think about theory

Changing how parents are involved in school after a process of consultation with the parents

Take time with colleagues to discuss purposes, values and roles

Challenging the problem identities of children and families and communities

Researching ways to consult with children

Respectful language

Trying again... and again to improve things

Realising that 'asking' is not enough

Consulting with the community on how to develop as an extended school

Having training in narrative practices

No blame

LISTEN

unities

LISTENING

Reducing rate of exclusion

Getting young people to research whether your service is effective

VOICE

A CULTURE OF PARTICIPATION

Seeing 'Kate' as a person not as a disability

Keeping hold of children

Helping parents so they don't have to battle for education provision

VOICE

Not calling for alternative placement

Talking to Tom' before the lesson as this helps him settle

Challenging curriculum

Changing services to deliver to individual family needs

CRITICAL REFLECTIVE PRACTICE

Challenging institutional racism positively

A solution approach

VALUING THE INDIVIDUAL

VOICE

Flexible curriculum

Deconstructing assumptions of practice

COLLABORATION

Learn about participation from SureStart

Working out what social constructionism means in practice

Look for signs of children learning and changing

VOICE

Changing the structure of meetings to enable the rich stores of children's identities to be available

THE SOLID WALL SUPPORTING INCLUSION

Collaborative working between children, young people, families and professionals is key to the government's long-term strategy to promote the well-being of children including more inclusive education, and is mentioned at least 40 times in *Every Child Matters* (HMSO, 2003).

> We intend, subject to consultation, to place a duty on all relevant local bodies (such as the police and health organisations) in exercising their normal functions, to have regard to safeguarding children, promoting their well-being and working together through local partnership arrangements (section 5.35: 81).

> The aim of these reforms is to organise services around the needs of children and young people. Achieving this is a shared responsibility between national, regional and local government, partners in the voluntary and private sectors and children, young people and families (section 5.57).

Participation is seen as crucial to the planning for integrated services in Scotland, and is linked to inclusivity:

> Those leading the children's services planning process must ensure that arrangements are inclusive and that, in particular, children, parents and relevant voluntary organisations are involved as full participants.
>
> (Scottish Executive, 2001: 77)

The need for multi-agency working co-ordinated by the school to tackle social inclusion is underlined in an interview with a head teacher of an extended school carried out in 2004:

> We had started to question the curriculum and our response was the social inclusion work which involves about 16% of the school population . . . we began to question also the effectiveness of the other services . . . it was our view that health, social services, police, drugs people, counselling services were all pulling in different directions and teachers were becoming social workers and they could never get social services when they wanted them, we were lucky if we saw any, we went through something like eleven educational psychologists in five years, there was no continuity, it was hopeless. Then there was a clear need to stabilise the whole situation because the one organisation which was stable in all of this was the school, all these others were whizzing around like horizontal yo-yos
>
> (From author's research; see Dyson, Millward and Todd, 2002)

The importance of partnership working for particular exclusions can also be identified from both research and policy documents. For example, the importance of different kinds of partnerships, but particularly multi-agency working and parent partnership, for special educational needs (SEN) inclusion is illustrated in a review of research on inclusion, where inclusion is thought of in terms of the education of children with special needs in mainstream schools:

> There was considerable emphasis on the importance of partnerships, particularly in relation to the role of support services, inter-agency co-operation and partnership with parents. LEAs, Health Authorities and Social Services, who have responsibility for children with SEN, worked under separate management systems and in non-overlapping areas, causing difficulties for effective inter-agency partnerships. Furthermore, these agencies could have different priorities and responsibilities in relation to pupils with SEN.
>
> (Ainscow *et al.*, 1999: 57–58)

In the development of cultural diversity, to reduce the exclusion of children from different ethnic groups, partnership working is again seen as important, defined here in terms of giving a voice:

> Most successful multi-ethnic schools have good relationships with, and listen to, parents and young people and were prepared to consider and debate values as well as strategies.
>
> (Richardson *et al.*, 1999)

For many researchers and practitioners, inclusion for all children means involving children and young people in decision-making – in other words, another kind of partnership working:

> If we are to design the best services for young people, we must learn to listen to them, value their opinion, and involve them in decision-making . . . our failure to listen to them can mean that services often exclude the very people who need them most . . . We had a fair idea of the adult agenda – for example concerns about the health and safety of children in relation to substance abuse or sexual behaviour, educational achievement, youth crime, etc. What we did not know was whether children and young people themselves shared this agenda, or whether another set of priorities existed.
>
> (Cairns, 2001: 349)

Partnership between children/young people, parents and professionals is clearly very important for the development of inclusion. The challenge is to move beyond the rhetoric that accompanies notions of 'partnership' to achieve ways of working that are experienced by all parties as collaborative. There are some clear issues to be addressed in all three areas of partnership:

- *Child and young person consultation and participation.* There have been major moves to consult with children and young people and to involve them more in schools and services. However, the child's voice is often absent from educational decisions that concern them. It is rarely heard in the deliberations of teachers, other professionals and policy-makers when trying to fashion education in a more inclusive guise.
- *Partnership with parents.* Parent partnership has been a mantra in education for many years now. There is now a massive range of initiatives to involve parents in education and they are involved to varying degrees when there are concerns about a child. However, there are few signs that they have any real influence in shaping education or any role in developing ways to make education more inclusive.
- *Multi-agency working.* You would be forgiven for thinking that the only concern for many professionals is multi-agency working. It is now central to policy and practice in children's services. However, it remains problematic. More importantly, it is not clear how far an improvement in the ways agencies and professionals work together will assist the development of inclusive education.

To move forward in developing greater understanding about these issues and to develop ideas about constructive actions, this book asks some key questions:

- What partnership is happening now? How are we involving children, young people and parents in the development of schools and in decision-making about use of services in education, health and social care? How are their voices being heard? How are children, young people and parents playing a collaborative role with professionals?
- What are the limits – gaps – and problems?
- What more can we understand about the link between partnership and inclusive education? How is collaborative working between children, young people and professionals and between parents

and professionals contributing to the development of inclusive education?

- How can we move forward? In what ways can people work together to facilitate inclusive education?

The answers to these questions – in the ensuing chapters – are based on extensive research. The author's research into parent and child partnership (Todd, 2000) and into extended schools (Cummings *et al.*, 2005) informs many of the chapters. A number of research projects from students working with the author, carried out for degrees or postgraduate qualifications, are also drawn upon and referenced throughout the book. In other areas existing research has been critically summarised, reflecting the value given to the presenting of ideas based on and informed by research.

The remaining sections of this chapter present some key understandings that inform the book. First, a note on terms defines some of the words that will be most likely overused in the coming chapters, words such as professional, practitioner and multi-agency. A separate section sets out the adoption of a wide and critical definition of inclusive education.

Professional . . . practitioner? Multi-agency . . . multi-professional? A note on terms

First, a clarification of how some over-used terms will be understood. The words 'professional', 'practitioner' and 'worker' are used throughout this book, often as if they were synonymous with each other. They are used to refer to all people placed in a role working to assist the welfare and development of children, young people and families, whether in a paid or voluntary role, whether working in services, voluntary agencies or schools. This includes teaching assistants, teachers, learning mentors, family support workers, educational welfare officers, nurses, consultants in community health, doctors, social workers, head teachers, educational psychologists, clinical psychologists, occupational therapists, physiotherapists, attendance officers, extended school co-ordinators, BEST team managers, Sure Start workers, project workers, adoption and fostering officers and so on. The list is potentially endless. 'Professional' can have a clear definition in terms of training and status accorded by a particular professional body, such as the General Medical Council (GMC) or the British Psychological Society (BPS), but that is not the case in how 'professional' is used here. Others working with children and families might not have and might not wish for such professional definition. Some people prefer to use the word 'practitioners' or 'workers' instead of 'professionals' and might find the inter-changeability of terms unhelpful. However, all three terms are used to acknowledge that, whether or not people working with children and families accept such status, the traits of professionalism are often accorded to them and the assumptions of professionalism remain as invitations open to them to take up in practice.

The term 'multi-agency' is used to refer to all the different ways that professionals, workers or practitioners occupying different roles might work together. Often texts make distinctions between inter-agency, multi-agency and multi-professional. However, in this book multi-agency is used to refer equally to when those of different agencies work together as when people work across agencies. When such distinctions are required they are made.

The meaning of 'partnership' is discussed throughout the book – and the evolution of an understanding of what this means is really a central purpose of the book. More will be said on this subject within this chapter. The context of partnership that is relevant to the concerns of this book is any and all kinds of interactions between practitioner/worker and children/young people and parents. This refers to interactions in schools and services, both formal and informal, planned and opportunistic, in the course of teaching in classrooms, consultation in services, and any activities in other projects, initiatives and organisations. The definition of inclusive education assumed throughout this book is discussed in the next section in this chapter. It is a broad definition, encompassing all pupils, not just those of particular groups, so broad that 'inclusion' is often used interchangeably with 'inclusive education'. One of the purposes of such an open definition is to enable the drawing out of characteristics of partnership that can facilitate inclusive education. Another, as will become clearer later in the chapter, is the centrality of the need to pull apart accepted terms and ideas in order to best understand their purposes and achievements in the lives of children, families and professionals.

Throughout this book use is made of the voices of children, young people, parents and professionals from different pieces of research. They are used to give more depth to points being made, and there is no attempt to try to represent the voices of all children/young people and adults. 'Parents' is used and can be assumed to mean parents and carers. 'Children' and 'young people' are often referred to separately, but are sometimes used interchangeably to prevent the continuous listing of all possible terms.

Inclusion: a broad inclusive concept

The pun is intended. One of the purposes of the term 'inclusive education' is, the author would suggest, to call into question some accepted understandings about how we 'do' schools, and how we think about education. When the term becomes a 'buzz word' – as is now the situation – it is perhaps the case that some of these challenges have become lost, and 'inclusive education' comes instead to mean something with clearer boundaries. This brings us back to our current need to start this book with an exploration of the kind of challenges that are meant by inclusive education.

This book challenges many current ideas and understandings of what inclusion is about. The post-structuralist idea of deconstruction leads to a questioning of who is being spoken of, who is the subject of 'exclusion' or 'inclusion', and what kind of education a child or young person is being excluded from or included in.

The definition of inclusion adopted by this book is one that encompasses all children and young people rather than selecting those from particular groups. We can easily collect evidence on any number of serious exclusions. We know that pupils who categorise themselves ethnically as White, Indian, Chinese, White/Asian and Irish are more likely to gain five or more A*–C GCSEs compared to other ethnic groups. Gypsy/Roma pupils, Travellers of Irish heritage and Black Caribbean pupils are amongst the lower achieving pupils at Key Stage 3 (DfES, 2005a). Permanent exclusion rates are higher than average for Travellers of Irish Heritage, Gypsy/Roma, Black Caribbean, Black Other and White/Black Caribbean pupils. Black Caribbean and Black Other boys are twice as likely to have been categorised as having behavioural, emotional or social difficulty as White British boys (identified as a special educational need type of School Action Plus or statement). These are all concerns relevant to inclusive education: children who by dint of their membership of certain groups are in some way excluded from educational opportunities.

However, this book avoids listing groups. There would always be a danger in forgetting about certain children. An organisation in Durham, Investing in Children, that works regionally and nationally to extend the participation of young people in developing the services that affect them, similarly resists 'the temptation to be drawn into exclusive debates about the position of particular groups of children and young people' (Cairns, 2001: 350). Like Cairns, this book adopts the belief that the most powerful arguments for change lie in a universal approach, listening to what all children say, and working for common goals. By considering needs of particular groups, the effect is to drive children's rights into a narrow cul-de-sac (Cairns, 2001: 351). Another effect is that children become defined by their group identity rather than their status as children. Cairns explains how an administrative convenience – demarcating children into groups – can serve to keep groups of children apart from one another (350–351). There is nevertheless a recognition that there are important things to be said by, as well as on behalf of, children who find themselves members of certain groups. It means that 'inclusive education' is not defined, in this book, by an analysis of the needs only of children associated with groups with currently defined exclusions. The following definition comes close, as it encompasses all:

> The notion of inclusion therefore does not set boundaries (as the notion of integration did) around particular kinds of supposed disability. Instead it is about providing a framework within which all children – regardless of ability, gender, language, ethnic or cultural origin – can be valued equally, treated with respect and provided with real opportunities at school.
>
> (Thomas and Loxley, 2001: 119)

The concept of inclusion adopted by this book is an active one – and it is critical – and not fixed. It has us all constantly asking questions about what it is. For example, any simple equating of inclusion with mainstream education is questioned. Such thinking can be restricting since it can position people outside 'inclusion'. For example, parents who reject a mainstream placement for their child can find themselves being seen as opposing inclusion, when what they are opposing, may be, for example, a lack of appropriate resources in a mainstream setting. A mainstream place definition of inclusion can also inaccurately place children inside inclusive education when they may in certain ways (for example, socially) be experiencing exclusion (Ainscow *et al.*, 1999; Watson *et al.*, 1999).

There is also an assumption or process – of actively changing or moving from something – in a critique of current situations or understandings, and towards alternatives. The Centre for Studies in Inclusive Education in Bristol also defines inclusion in a way that both challenges various existing understandings and takes a process approach – 'the gradual transfer of resources, expertise, staff and students to an appropriately supported, diverse and inclusive mainstream' – as its method of achieving a political goal: 'Desegregated education . . . a crucial first step in helping to change discriminatory attitudes, in creating greater understanding and in developing a fairer society' (CISE, 2003a).

Away from discrimination, towards diversity and social justice. In this there is a clear assumption that inclusive education is not just about schools. There is a range of ideas about what the wider context has to do with inclusive education. One idea is that educational inequalities are to be understood as having been created by the culture and society as a whole, which encompasses schools but is also beyond the school gates:

> answers to questions about 'why children fail' might lie as much in the social, economic and political structures of a society as in anything intrinsic to children or 'lacking' in a child. From a critical theorist's viewpoint, it becomes easier to question the deficit model of children, which assumes that negative properties for his or her educational failure. It becomes easier to examine the social processes by which 'achievement' is defined. Who, for example, decides what achievement is in a society where the highest achievers are almost always white, upper- or middle-class males? Why does being a poor reader and working class seem to have much more serious and long-term social consequences than being a poor reader and upper or middle class?
>
> (Tomlinson, 1982)

The message is that we need ways to understand one aspect of educational inclusion – educational achievement or failure – with respect to society and culture as a whole. The corollary of this is that educational exclusions become the domain of services other than education, and, taking this further, that exclusions other than in education – in fact all exclusions – become the concerns of all. This is the now common 'joined-up' thinking. Ainscow's definition encompasses some of these ideas:

> My current approach is to define inclusive education as a process of increasing the participation of pupils in, and reducing their exclusion from, the cultures, curricula and communities of their local schools, not forgetting, of course, that education involves many processes that occur outside of schools.
>
> (Ainscow, 1999: 218)

It is therefore not surprising that the DfES policy on inclusion is now very much an integration of educational and social inclusion – the focus solely on special needs and disability has disappeared. Coined in the 1960s in France, the concept of 'social exclusion' became common terminology in government policy speak when the Social Exclusion Unit was established in 1997. 'Social exclusion' is defined by New Labour as:

> a shorthand term for what can happen when people or areas suffer from a combination of linked problems such as unemployment, poor skills, low incomes, unfair discrimination, poor housing, high crime, bad health and family breakdown.
>
> (ODPM, 2004)

More recently, schools have been identified as one of the main locations for the delivery of integrated services – in both England and Scotland. The Green Paper *Every Child Matters* (HMSO, 2003) and the Children Act 2004 embody a focus on social inclusion by looking to a fundamental rearrangement of services as a way to meet five outcomes for children around being healthy, staying safe, enjoying life, achieving, making a positive contribution, and economic well-being (HMSO, 2003: 6–7). The intention is:

> That every child has the chance to fulful their potential by reducing levels of educational failure, ill health, substance misuse, teenage pregnancy, abuse and neglect, crime and anti-social behaviour among children and young people.

Policy in Scotland bears similarities. This serves to further reinforce the importance of schools in working collaboratively and strategically with all family and child services and with the community outside the school to meet the needs of children and help address the societal issues that can manifest as barriers to both social and educational inclusion. Chapter 5 develops ideas about how social inclusion is – or is not – furthered though integrated services.

In widening an understanding of inclusive education there is a danger that what goes on in schools is forgotten. There is an open challenge to continually question who, in a school, can take part and what kind of role are they able to play, and who cannot take part or play certain roles – and what is offered in the school as 'education' that children are being included in or excluded from. Changes in what passes as education, via changes in pedagogy, also lead schools further towards inclusion:

Thinking skills approaches provide powerful pedagogical strategies that constitute a manageable unit of change and support teachers in the development of a classroom climate conducive to transformative learning and the promotion of democratic relationships.

(Baumfield, 2003: 179)

Some writers argue that without a wide and critical definition of inclusion, inclusive education might actually result in more exclusion. It is useful to draw on Viet-Wilson's weak vs. strong version of exclusion, quoted by Macrae, 'a weak version merely attempts to include the excluded, a "strong" version addresses the mechanisms through which powerful constituencies exercise their capacity to exclude' (Macrae, 2003). Here 'strong' is 'a critical approach'. A critical approach to inclusive education requires a deconstruction of current ways of thinking about the term and the concept; it needs thinking that is 'outside the box' in order to (repeating an earlier quote) '(provide) a framework within which all children – regardless of ability, gender, language, ethnic or cultural origin – can be valued equally, treated with respect and provided with real opportunities at school (Thomas and Loxley, 2001: 119). Tinkering with what we have now can only go so far. We may even need new terms to replace 'inclusive education' or 'inclusion' or 'partnership'. Slee (1996) has argued that so far schools have failed to alter their culture and practices in order to increase pupil participation and remove exclusionary pressures, suggesting that 'inclusion, a euphemism for containment and assimilation, ignores the need for deconstruction and recognition across a range of boundaries' (Allen, 1999: 11). Allen arrives at the following definition:

Inclusive education is about responding to diversity; it is about listening to unfamiliar voices, being open, empowering all members and about celebrating 'difference' in dignified ways. From this perspective, the goal is not to leave anyone out of school.

(Allen, 1999: 14)

and:

The solution [to educational inclusion] lies in developing social policy that promotes negotiation between adults and children and recognises the ability of children, families and service providers to develop their own localised solutions to their everyday life problems.

(Davis *et al.*, 2003: 207)

No inclusion without participation

Education, and the external services that support it in various ways, cannot respond to diversity unless the system is able to hear unfamiliar voices. Throughout this book, a key assumption is that inclusive education requires ways to hear the voices of children, young people, parents and professionals – and, as a result, have action taken. Education cannot be inclusive without collaborating with children and parents in ways that enable their perspectives to influence the development of schools and systems. Partnership is central to inclusion. Therefore, there is a remaining definition essential to the concerns of this book – that of partnership.

This book is, in effect, a story exploring how we can think about partnership. Partnership is an over-used term in education and other services for children – so much used that its meaning is be in danger of becoming lost. Indeed, it is likely to have a range of meanings. There are a number of terms that have related concerns – such as 'consultation', 'involvement', giving a 'voice', 'participation' and 'collaboration'. As a short-hand, and to avoid continually being tentative about terms, 'participation' is often used in this book. It assumes the role of signalling that what is spoken about is more than lip-service, is more than asking opinions and not acting on them, that the voice of the other is given more centrality and has a greater part to play. However, all these terms are lifted up and examined, then put back in different ways, like the long process of weeding a tightly packed overgrown garden.

Along the way discoveries are made about what kinds of relationships we might need to try to develop so that inclusion for all children is assisted. For example, in Chapter 2 a distinction arises between 'consultation' and 'participation' and it is here that the preference for 'participation' emerges. 'Partnership' is invoked regularly as a critical device. In Chapters 2 and 3 the kinds of relationships that children have with public life and with the schools and services they experience is examined to tease out what is happening – what kinds of participation are, or are not, happening. In Chapter 4, the nature of partnership in 'parent partnership' is subject to critique. Chapter 5 explores how far different aims of the kinds of partnership that happen between professionals are consistent with these professionals playing a role in inclusive education. Integrated services brings particular opportunities for such partnerships, and Chapter 5 considers whether this similarly invites inclusion. And in Chapters 6 and 7 the PPC (Practice–People–Context) Model of professional practice is developed that arises from preceding chapters. This model suggests that there are available to us a range of understandings of practice that have different implications for the kinds of relationships possible between practitioners, children/young people and parents. It also tries to demonstrate the kinds of relationships that might count as participation for inclusive education.

Some ideas that are assumed by this exploration of partnership

This book draws on a range of theoretical ideas to make sense of why participation seems to be difficult to bring about. These ideas are introduced in the ensuing paragraphs, developed in the following chapters and returned to in Chapter 6, when the concluding understandings about participation are brought together. But first a note on why any theory is needed. One of the assumptions of this book is that it is possible to develop a practical theory that provides a critical approach to professional practice – and one of the book's aims is to contribute to this. With a critical approach to practice, the practitioner/ worker is able to have a firm foundation for action. With the theoretical background, actions take place with understanding. Unexpected outcomes can be analysed in order to know how they came about, and how to reproduce them if such outcomes are what is wanted. Without the practical, the theoretical is an empty vessel. This book aims to communicate tough ideas in an accessible format by introducing theories that give practical tools to assist busy professionals. Above all, it aims to go much further than the descriptive or the surface. The kinds of understandings that follow are consistent with a community psychology approach (King and Wilson, 2006; MacKay, 2006; Kagan *et al.*, 2006). The theories are presented as 'ideas'.

Ideas about the individual perspectives of people

It is both an assumption of this book and a finding that people – children, young people and adults – are able to communicate their perspectives, and that these perspectives bear witness to unique personal stories. These unique perspectives cannot be assumed by knowing certain things about a person such as their age, level of education, class, ethnicity, status as disabled or not. Much of the research drawn upon throughout this book accessed the voices of children, young people, parents and professionals and it is these perceptions that are used to develop ideas about what is needed in order to make collaborative working relationships more possible. These ideas draw on social constructionist and post-structuralist understandings that look for different perspectives to bear witness to social practices.

Ideas about how we actively construct and make sense of events that we experience

When professionals work with children and parents they actively make sense of these interactions. Meaning is given to what they experience. Similarly, parents and children/young people make active sense of their interactions with professionals. In other words, ideas of social constructivism are assumed in what happens between professionals, children and parents. Such ideas also come from socio-cultural psychology which looks at human beings as active participants in the world. Children are not passive recipients of parenting or learning: they want to shape the way they are parented and taught. This is evident, particularly in the ideas presented in Chapter 3, about how professionals present themselves to children. In Chapter 3 we consider what children make of professionals and the potentially disastrous consequences for children of what are essentially misunderstandings on both sides. Social constructivist ideas are also implicit in Chapter 4, when the repercussions of deficit and normative conceptualisations of parents for partnership are explored.

Ideas about the importance of understanding events in terms of the wider social, cultural and political context

The exploration of how we think about inclusive education has already brought to the fore the importance of understanding what happens in education as a function of the social and cultural context. It follows that we are likely only to unravel partnership, make heads and tails of its successes, failures and ways forward, if we conceptualise what happens between people, say a teacher and a child, or a doctor and a parent, in the wider context in which these relationships take place. So, whether educational psychologists are able to involve children in their consultations, and whether teachers are able to develop partnership with parents, requires us to see these interactions in their full complexity: as actions that take place within complex institutions and within a society that brings its influences to bear in every hidden corner of experience.

All the thinking in this book is premised, both implicitly and explicitly at different times, on grasping what it means to understand action and experience as a function of context. In Chapter 3 children's levels of participation in all services they use, health, welfare and education, are assumed to have some impact on their involvement in the development of inclusive education. The kind of inclusion that is possible in schools has some connection with the way professionals who operate outside school interact with children and young people. For example, inclusion within school of children looked after by public care is likely to be strongly influenced by the attention given by social services to the educational needs of children. When children attending school become known, due to a concern, to external services, the way these services respond to children is likely to have some impact on the kinds of inclusion possible for these children. And finally, the different cultures of collaboration that particular services and schools develop with children and young people are likely to influence each other.

Context also refers to the historical legacy of institutions, central to Bourdieu's *habitus* (see Chapter 6). We cannot understand what kinds of partnerships between children, young people, parents and professionals are needed to develop inclusive education without taking into consideration the history of the development of relationships between families and schools. As an example of this, in Chapter 4, the way partnership with parents is understood is given a brief historical review.

In Chapter 5, the ways the complex context of different professional groups influences how they can work together with each other for inclusion is explored using a tool of socio-cultural theory, an activity system. Activity theorists assume that the basic unit of analysis of human behaviour is not seen to be within the individual or even within the immediate situation between those involved, but is at the level of an activity system. Often we exclude, in our thinking, the relationship between the persons' acting and the setting. Activity theory says that human action is socially constituted and given meaning by its location in societally, historically and politically generated systems of activity. An activity system puts human activity into the social, political, historical and economic context in which it occurs – asking for a consideration of the whole context in order to understand practice. These ideas have developed from a particular tradition of post-Vygotskian psychologists including Engestrom, Leont'ev and Wertsch. Engestrom has devised a way of modelling human activity, in the form of an activity system, that maps out the different complex aspects of a context, and enables us to understand more about what is happening and about how to achieve desired changes (Daniels, 2001; Engestrom, 1996; Engestrom, 1999; Engestrom *et al.*, 1999). In Chapter 5 there is an example of using an activity system to deconstruct the potential for inclusion in one aspect of integrated services.

Central to 'context' is how we understand people and the ideas that make up how we think about professional practice. These have a crucial impact on the kinds of working relationships that are possible. It is to these that we turn to next.

Ideas that we need to deconstruct social practices if we are going to develop participation with children/young people and parents

Social constructionism involves the idea that the social world, including ourselves, is the product of social and cultural processes.

> The social environment is not separate from people – as might be assumed when we talk of the influence of the environment on behaviour, for example. Human beings together construct the social world, but they are not free to construct it in any image they choose, because they are born into a world that has already been constructed in a particular way by their predecessors. This constructed social world then assumes the status of an objective reality for successive generations of people. Berger and Luckmann express this continuous, circular process thus: Society is a human product, Society is an objective reality. Man [*sic*] is a social product.
>
> (Burr, 2002: 79)

There are a number of ideas that follow from this that underlie the deliberations of this book. A key idea is that professional practice is not immune from this construction:

> Post-structuralist thinking encourages professionals to see professional practice, as all social life, as constructed, and to deconstruct in order to reflect on how to develop enabling practice. We can think of society as a text, like a book, that can be read. What we would look for in order to read society would be constructed ideas – the themes, narratives, discourses – that come to be given the status of 'truths' that are around us, in the 'ether'. They are beliefs we may not even really realise we have about how things

are and how things should be. They are simple and complex; they are contradictory and change all the time, yet they are ever present. These truths construct norms around which persons are invited to shape or constitute their lives. Therefore these are 'truths' that actually specify persons' lives (White and Epston, 1990: 21). This is a different understanding of what power is about – as, 'Power is actively (re-) produced in discourse' (Billington, 2000: 59).

(Todd, 2006: 147)

There are norms (social practices, discourses) and assumptions that come to be seen as fact, that form the backdrop to how we are in the world as people: as practitioners/workers. Some norms – for example of gender, ethnicity, class, disability and sexuality – call us into narrow conclusions in terms of group identities. Some discourses of professional practice – such as having expert knowledge and constructing problems and their solution in terms of the medical model (to name just two examples) – call professionals into certain ways of seeing people with whom they work and certain kinds of relationships with clients. Understandings of what it means to be a child or a parent similarly restrict how we see a child or a parent. It is not that we necessarily choose these – they are part of society. If we want to work with children/young people and parents – in schools and services – in ways that develop collaborative working relationships, we may need to examine some of these norms, discourses and conceptualisations of professional practice. The need for such an examination becomes an essential task as the analysis of partnership develops through the chapters of this book. In Chapters 2 and 3, ideas about what it means to be a child and understandings of professional practice are suggested to have implications for invitations for the participative opportunities available. Similarly, in Chapter 4, current assumptions of 'parent' and 'family', when combined with certain discourses of professional practice, make parent partnership highly problematic. In Chapter 6, we return again to these theoretical ideas and a practical model (the PPC, Practice–People–Context, Model) to help us to challenge social practices that do not fit with collaborative working relationships.

Ideas that language is active – it does not just stand for something, it does something

One way to be aware of the social practices of professional/practitioner/ worker roles is to deconstruct language. Language, according to social constructionism, is not regarded merely as standing in for something: words are active and play a role in creating identity. When a child is born and the midwife announces, 'it is a girl!', she is not merely being descriptive. Her language indicates that gender is an important category, and gender is marked out as having meaning. From then on much around us asserts that gender is important, and we devote a lot of time to learning how to be a 'boy' or a 'girl' – even if we react against the prevailing gender norms, such norms are still defining. The existence of politically correct terms, whatever one's view of their use, underlines the perspective that different ways of using language have different senses and meanings. 'A disabled person' suggests the disability is integral to the person, and the person cannot be seen separate from the disability. A 'person with disabilities' is more likely to enable the person to be considered first and the disability to be understood as one aspect of the person.

All the terms of inclusion and partnership, such as 'diversity', 'exclusion', 'need', 'difficulty', 'assessment', 'consultation' and even 'partnership' and 'inclusive education', are all constructed terms. They have all come about over time, responding to a complex set of needs. If we unravel these terms – or deconstruct them – this can assist a constructive search for the kind of society that fits with our values, hopes and purposes – in the case of this book, this means one that develops an effective enabling inclusive education. This process of identifying discourses, of reading life as texts, is referred to as deconstruction, from a cultural literary theorist, Derrida, and is a key tool of a post-structuralist approach to inclusive education:

> A deconstruction is a process of critical reading and unravelling of terms, loaded terms and tensions between terms that construct how we read our place in culture and in our families and in our relationships, and how we think about who we are and what it might be possible for us to be.
>
> (Parker, 1999: 6–7)

For example, the concepts of 'needs' and 'special needs', crucial to one way of thinking about inclusion, can be investigated to find out what they are doing for children and teachers. What other terms and ideas do they help to support? How did they come into being? This kind of questioning is what is known as deconstruction in post-structuralism. It involves a taking apart of assumptions. When we look at 'need' we already know that it is a circular and relative term. The legislation refers to children's special needs as relative to those of other children in the same locality, and with reference to efficient use of resources, rather than the need having some objective definition of its own. What one school regards as a special need will not be seen in the same way by another school when there are very different levels of relative achievement in two schools. Woodhead (1991) has suggested that the label 'need' carries a lot of power. It is very hard to argue against something that is presented as a need, arguably more so if that need is presented as special, as it carries the flavour of 'rights'. I asked several groups of professionals, including teachers, psychologists and speech therapists, to carry out an exercise in which they questioned 'need' and thought about what it was doing in the world. They discovered that 'need' suggests powerlessness on the part of those who have the need and that others, experts, must do the defining of needs. They noted that a whole army of professionals and industry of technologies (tests, training, books) have grown up around the defining of need. It always, they noted, signals something not right about the person in 'need' – a deficit model of the client. The use of 'need', and particularly 'special need' made professionals feel they were doing some good in helping people feel better. It seemed to help us keep our jobs as there would always be someone required to define and meet 'need'. The different professionals could not see a time when there would not be need. This is not to suggest that there are not real problems in schools. Such a post-structuralist deconstruction of 'need' allows us to think about whether 'need' and 'special needs' are helpful concepts. We can consider what interests are being served. It allows a critical questioning that might find different and more helpful ways of thinking about the difficulties people experience. In terms of the interests of this book, critical thinking about all the terms and practices of work enables us to understand why partnership is problematic. It enables us to discover which beliefs, theories and tools – which ways of thinking about our roles, about the nature of problems, about children and about families – to use and develop so as to encourage greater collaborative practice.

Now read and enjoy the book. Browse Chapters 2 and 3 to reflect on practice that brings about the participation of children and young people, Chapter 4 for a critical consideration of parent partnership, and Chapter 5 to look again at multi-agency working. The PPC (Practice–People–Context) Model of participative inclusive professional practice is considered in Chapter 6, with case study examples of practice in Chapter 7.

2 Being seen and heard and making a difference

How children participate

It's nice to know that some teachers want to know how we feel about learning.

(Nicole, year 6, in Flutter and Ruddock, 2004: 13)

Children have changed, and schools should!

(Lynda, 16, in Burke and Grosvenor, 2003: 1)

I think teachers should be a little bit barmy and dance and not just sit down and drink tea and coffee.

(Kirsty, 10, in Burke and Grosvenor, 2003: 83)

Cos we know more than adults. Some children are more brave minded than adults. So that big people can see things from a little kid's eyes.

(Tolley *et al.*, 1998: 25)

There has been a major increase over the last five to ten years of youth organisations that involve children and young people in the planning and running of activities. Children have also been heard in public decision-making in a variety of different kinds of organisations – including schools. The DfES commissioned a snapshot of participation to find out what was happening for young people living in England in Spring 2003 (Cutler and Taylor, 2003). This showed:

[a] huge and welcome increase in the level of activity by almost all organisations in the last five years to involve young people in decision-making. However, it is early days and therefore it is natural to see a great range in the level of development of organisations in putting in place the essential infrastructure for effective practice.

(Cutler and Taylor, 2003: 107)

The DfES also commissioned a survey of good practice in the participation of children and young people in schools, organisations and services (Kirby *et al.*, 2003b). Using existing databases such as the National Youth Agency (NYA) and the networks of the National Children's Bureau (NCB), this survey established a list of almost 150 organisations which had involved children and young people in policy development, service delivery or evaluation. Twenty-nine agencies were selected as case studies and were investigated through documentary evidence, and through group and individual interviews with children, young people and adults. This has enabled good practice to be conceptualised and a development handbook for organisations to be published (Kirby *et al.*, 2003a). Similar work has been commissioned in health services (DH, 2002). This chapter draws upon such surveys and other research literature to explore:

- What partnership is going on? How are children and young people becoming involved in schools, services and research?
- Why consult? Why develop participation? What are the benefits?
- What are the best methods of consultation and participation to use?
- What are the key issues?

This chapter is an overview of the current developments. In Chapter 3 one aspect of child participation that emerges from this chapter is unpicked and examined in more detail. The aim of Chapter 3 is to find out more about children's perspectives on the services they use: what do they understand of the roles and purposes of the professionals they consult? What is the extent to which practitioners approach children as partners when they use services? In Chapter 7 the work of one organisation – Investing in Children – that promotes the participation of children and young people in public life is presented as a case study. The kinds of services children/young people might want, a starting point for any exploration that readers may undertake, a joint venture with the children/young people who use readers' services or attend your schools, is collated from research and presented in the Appendix.

What partnership is going on?

The last few years has seen a massive increase in the interest of public services in the participation of children and young people. This has developed partly through policy moves to reduce social exclusion and increase citizenship at the same time as being prepared to make radical changes to services. Children and young people have a strong wish to be consulted (Ruegger, 2001; Stafford *et al.*, 2003), particularly on issues directly affecting their daily lives and activities. Children regard being heard as a right:

> they did not seem to regard the opportunity to be heard as a favour for which they should be grateful. Rather, it was something they regarded as a right, they were willing to engage in if it served some useful purpose. It was a job to be done to achieve a better deal for themselves and young people.
>
> (Stafford *et al.*, 2003: 365–366)

Children are also well able to comment on what they see as good participation and on ways their voice can be better heard by adults in professional roles (Lightfoot and Sloper, 2003a; Stafford *et al.*, 2003; Tolley *et al.*, 1998; Armstrong *et al.*, 2000). The perspectives of children and young people as documented in research, some of it carried out by children, are referred to in this chapter.

Child consultation on policy

A commitment to child/young person participation at the level of the state and local authority has been signalled in a number of ways:

- Commissioners for children have been appointed: in Wales (Comisiynydd Plant Cymru) in December 2000, in Scotland in 2004, in Northern Ireland in 2003 and in England in March 2005. Enabling the voice of the child to be heard is an explicit aspect of the role of all three.
- The government has sought children's opinions on policy and legislation via questionnaires and focus groups. National policy consultations with children have included one on the Green Paper *Every Child Matters*, the *National Service Framework for Children* (NSFC), and the DfES Green Paper on extending opportunities and raising/Standards for 14- to 19-year-olds (DfES, 2002). Members of the government consulted with young people via a tour of England (Dixon *et al.*, 2003), and the DfES has also consulted on consultation itself – asking when and how children and young people should be called on for their views of services. Indeed, for the 'every child matters' agenda the government not only produced a document summarising children's responses to the consultation, but also a document that says what is going to be done as a response to children's views (DfES, 2004b).
- National moves to re-organise services finds a requirement to

consult with children high on the agenda. In evolving a strategy for integrated services in Scotland, the Action Team sought to meet extensively with children and young people (Scottish Executive, 2001). *Every Child Matters* includes, in the executive summary, an explicit, on-going requirement to consult with children and young people in service development (HMSO, 2003: 10): 'real service improvement is only attainable through involving children and young people and listening to their views'.

- The National Service Framework Standards for Children, which sets out standards for the delivery of health services for children, has a number of core standards that are concerned with the need for children and their families to have an active role in the services they receive and to contribute to service development: 'Children and young people and their families need to participate actively in designing services and in providing feedback on the care they received' (DH and DfES, 2004, 2.3: 89).

- Many local authorities now have youth parliaments and support school councils. Whilst these can be tokenistic and by no means an easy answer for how to involve children, it still represents a notable attempt to put consultation into school and service priorities.

At one stage, according to the DfES surveys, 21 major government initiatives provided opportunities for children to influence decision-making at a local level (Kirby *et al.*, 2003b: 20). There were examples of both the funding of one-off consultations with children by strategic organisations, and the requirement by strategic organisations that funded agencies to demonstrate on-going dialogue with children (Kirby *et al.*, 2003b: 103).

Research on and with children and young people

There is an increase in research that seeks to find out children's per-spectives (Hamill and Boyd, 2003; Blatchford, 1996a; Mooney and Blackburn, 2003; Barker *et al.*, 2003; Hancock and Mansfield, 2002; Vernon *et al.*, 2003). This research is carried out by academics in HEIs and published in academic or practitioner journals, and by organisations in order to improve service delivery. Organisations sometimes use research that involves children to develop information for them – particular products or resources (i.e. CD-ROMS, informa-tion leaflets). Such research can be one-off events, meetings, interviews or questionnaires.

Some universities are becoming centres of creative practice in child participation, including the Open University Children's Research Centre and the Norah Fry Research Centre at Bristol University. The former describes its role:

> Our primary objective is to empower children and young people as active researchers. The CRC recognises that children are experts on their own lives. We value the child's perspective and believe in promoting child voice by supporting children to carry out research on topics that are important to them. The CRC is based at the Open University in Milton Keynes. We offer diverse groups of children and young people a taught programme on all aspects of the research process followed by one-to-one support to design and carry out a research project. We also help them to disseminate their research findings, support a variety of outreach programmes. It links to numerous schools and community organisations and exists to contribute to the body of knowledge on childhood and children's views.
>
> (http://childrens-research-centre.open.ac.uk/ Feb 2006)

Rather than carrying out research on or about young people there is a move towards their direct involvement as researchers (Clark *et al.*, 2001; Morris, 2002; Morris, 1998; Cairns, 2001). This is central to the Open University Children's Research Centre. Once again voluntary agencies, for whom this is the major function or a key aspect of their work, have developed professional capacity, a variety of methodologies and time to facilitate this kind of work. Child/young person involvement in research needs to become a central focus in order for it to happen successfully, and attract time and resources, and this has not often been built in to the kinds of research carried out at universities. A related movement in research has been to investigate children's perspectives on participation and on the methods used by adults to consult with them (Garth and Aroni, 2003; Stafford *et al.*, 2003), and an exploration of new methodology for participation (Lightfoot and Sloper, 2003a; Morris, 2002; Punch, 2002).

Child participation in schools and other organisations

Children have shown themselves able to voice opinions on all aspects of school and organisational life with clear and varied views of what they would like to see (Billington and Pomerantz, 2004; Burke and Grosvenor, 2003; Flutter and Ruddock, 2004).

When consulted pupils identify a number of key features they would want in schools: respect, fairness, autonomy, intellectual challenge, social support and security. Pupils are interested in changing structures that cast them in a marginal role. They want autonomy; they want school to be fair; they want to be individuals; they want to be important. School should be seen as a whole experience, not just lessons.

(Hobbs, 2005)

In terms of an institutional framework for participation, Ofsted (2003) now looks for a school to 'seek to involve pupils in its work and development', assessing the extent to which a school 'seeks, values and acts on pupils' views' (Ofsted, 2003: 43). In terms of the development of schools towards inclusion, the 'Index for Inclusion', widely used by schools, asks schools to assess whether account is being taken of the views of their pupils.

Schools councils amount to one of the few common approaches used in many schools to provide a vehicle for pupil consultation and participation. In some schools this leads to pupils being able to voice their opinions and achieve change (Cummings *et al.*, 2005). However, there is wide experience that school councils can still be adult managed, that the areas in which children are allowed to voice opinions for change are prescribed for them by teachers, that they do not enable the voice of all pupils to be heard and they all have variable claims to represent the pupil voice (Cairns and Brannon, 2005; Alderson, 2000).

One area often omitted from the scrutiny of school councils is what happens in the classroom in terms of the organisation of teaching and learning. In education, children's involvement in teaching and learning in schools has been supported by a major ESRC research programme, 'Consulting Pupils about Teaching and Learning' (Flutter and Ruddock, 2004) and other examples can be found (Kirby *et al.*, 2003b; McGuiness, 1998; Hart, 1996). Whilst Fielding (2001) finds some examples of transformative participation in learning, evidence suggests current understandings of what learning is about and current 'conditions for learning' (Rudduck and Flutter, 2000) in schools work against this happening in any widespread manner. Baumfield explores the conditions required to make teaching and learning a more collaborative process: using thinking skills in RE, with teacher development supported by a university research network (Baumfield, 2002; see also Chapter 7). There also is a history in schools of children acting as tutors to each other, in peer-tutoring schemes (Topping,

1995), but the manner in which this is conducted is generally directed by teachers with little consultation or participation with pupils.

Pupil involvement in the social and behavioural aspect of school life find some examples in current practice. One of the most widespread initiatives of this kind is pupil recruitment as peer counsellors, often as a way of countering bullying in schools (Cowie and Wallace, 2000; Topping, 1996). However, pupils are usually trained according to the adult views of how such systems should work, rather than participating themselves in the development of peer-counselling schemes. Kirby *et al.* (2003b: 103) give the example in one school of the development of a 'bully box' in which children can place their written concerns for teachers. The school case studies investigated by Kirby *et al.* also used regular peer-support activities to help children develop responsibility and autonomy about personal care and relationships (Kirby *et al.*, 2003b).

The school improvement movement, in evidence since the late 1980s, represents a missed opportunity to have started the involvement of pupils in changing all aspects of school (Hobbs, 2005). A more recent form of whole-school development, full-service extended schools, aiming (amongst other things) to provide a range of services on school site, shows evidence (Cummings *et al.*, 2005) of participation in the development and operation of some of the extended school activities and provisions, but no evidence of participation at the strategic level. Participation examples include school councils whose brief is widened, pupil consultation with the community (i.e. taking clipboards out onto the street and into shops and other community settings to consult about a school-community garden), consulting with all pupils in the school about organisational issues (i.e. a possible change in the timings of the school day), meetings for pupils to deliver views of activities to outside providers of out-of-school-hours activities, and many examples in which pupils developed initiatives themselves supported by members of staff. The latter include pupils working with the community to set up a community cinema, pupils developing a cycling proficiency course, the Key Fund initiative in which small groups of pupils prepare and present bids for funding their own projects to a group of outside professionals. Case studies demonstrating young people's participation in regeneration initiatives are documented by the Neighbourhood Renewal Unit (2006).

Several extended schools speak of being committed to pupil involvement and indeed several involve pupils in a large number of ways. However, there is no overall game plan for pupil participation, no involvement in the strategy for extended schools, no involvement in how the school is developing its espoused overall commitment to inclusion, or with processes to achieve inclusion such as the targeting of service delivery to pupils who cause concern. Such criticisms are not only levelled at extended schools. There is some evidence of consultation, but there is little evidence in schools generally of participation in anything other than isolated activities. Wyse (2001) found children well able to articulate complex issues but very limited in opportunities to have their perspectives listened to in the context of the school. He quotes a child saying, 'the most choice we ever get is which felt pen to use' (2001). There is a need for schools to find ways to involve children more authentically both in their own learning, in aspects of school life, and also more strategically in the development of school policy.

Children with special needs are now able to have a greater role in decision-making about individual education plans and about action taken about school placement. This is as a result of detailed guidelines for such involvement in the Code of Practice (DfES, 2001b; DfES, 2001a). Pupils experiencing difficulties at school, who have special arrangements made for them, have shown themselves well able to comment on their experience of themselves and on their educational environment (Owen *et al.*, 2004; Watson *et al.*, 1999; Connor, 2000; Allen, 1999; Frederickson *et al.*, 2004; Madge and Fassam, 1982; Rudduck and Flutter, 2000). A theme in some of this research is the resistance to being treated as different, ambivalence on the part of children with a disability to the disabled identity, and a need to be seen as a child or young person with concerns in common with other young people (Allen, 1999; Watson *et al.*, 1999). However, there is little research documenting the response of professionals to their perspectives. There is also little comprehensive research on the extent of pupil involvement in decision-making. Research that looks at the experience of young people of educational decision-making strongly suggests that they are rarely placed in the situation where they understand the role of the professional or where they can have an active role (Armstrong, 1995; Armstrong *et al.*, 1999; Galloway *et al.*, 1994; Gimrax and Bell, 2004; Sandbaek, 1999). Chapter 3 carefully explores this area.

There is more evidence of participatory activity in the voluntary sector than in schools, in which children and young people seem to be involved in decision-making within the organisations themselves, rather than in limited prescribed activities (Cutler and Taylor, 2003; Kirby *et al.*, 2003b). Organisations such as the Children's Society, National Children's Bureau, Barnardo's, British Youth Council, Save the Children, National Youth Agency, NSPCC, Triangle, Investing in Children, Young Voice, and the Carnegie Trust UK Youth Project have been engaging with children and young people in participation projects and building up a wealth of experience and publications that reflect this. Some of these focus on a particular area (i.e. journalism) but place a high value on the use of a participatory approach. Others exist to develop consultation itself, to set up and support groups of young people that various local strategic organisations access when wanting to consult young people. Many voluntary organisations now involve children and young people at the highest levels of decision-making in the way a particular project runs, or in the operation of the agency itself, showing that it is possible for young people and adults to work together on complex issues. There has also been the development of organisations run by or with children and young people, for example Article 12, UK Youth Parliament and Children's Express (Kirby *et al.*, 2003b: 26). Many voluntary organisations therefore play an important role in acting as a catalyst for participation by young people in services, schools and other statutory organisations.

Why consult? Why develop participation? What are the benefits?

The benefits of consulting with children and enabling participation have been claimed for the child themselves, for the adults in the organisation in which participation takes place and also for the organisational culture as a whole.

I will start, appropriately, with what children say they see as benefits. There is a desire for consultation to lead to some kind of change, but realism about what is possible. Children/young people say they think it is important for them to be given feedback summarising their views and the possibilities of change. They want to know their views have made some difference (Lightfoot and Sloper, 2003a). There is little research into the tangible outcomes of consultation and participation – on whether it has led to any changes in services or schools. Sloper and Lightfoot (2002) found that 17 of the 24 health initiatives where child participation had been identified reported changes in services as a result of consultation. Outcomes from seven initiatives included changes to hospital environment, ward décor and recreation facilities. In four there were changes to food on the ward and to ward routines, and in two there were changes in clinic times. Eleven went beyond consultation to involve children and young people in decision-making about service development. Feedback to children was reported in thirteen cases: seven gave a report on ongoing progress so far, four gave children tangible evidence of outcomes, and two gave a copy of the project report. A children's human rights project in Durham, 'Investing in Children' has seen many changes as a result of its projects, just one being better transport services for children in Durham (Cairns, 2001). The ways of working and the impact of young people's work with Investing in Children is considered again in Chapter 7. The government has started to publish its own responses to consultations with children, in the document *Every Child Matters . . . and Every Young Person. What You Said and What We're Going to Do* (DfES, 2004b).

This book assumes the importance of pupil involvement for the development of inclusive education. Salient examples of inclusion come from responses to diversity from listening to and acting on unfamiliar voices. Education and services will change in response to the active involvement of children, young people and parents. Hayes (2002) has taken this analysis further by articulating, both in terms of theory and practice, how it is that participation links to inclusive education. He suggests the advantages to pupils from collaboration in an inclusive school can be understood in terms of the enhancement of 'social capital' (Table 2.1). Social capital, from Bourdieu (1986), is a 'social structural resource' that serves as 'a capital asset for the individual' and facilitates certain actions and outcomes for those who occupy a given social structure (Coleman, 1990: 302). Unlike other forms of capital, it is not possessed by individuals but exists in the relationships between individuals and it is characterised by mutual trust and an expectation of reciprocity. 'Trust, obligations and expectations, norms, relations of authority and shared information are all examples of social capital because they are resources that arise from the social relations of individuals who share membership in a common social structure' (Carbanaro, 1998: 296). It can be suggested that participation, via incremental social capital, is an important way to improve social inequalities.

The benefits of consultation are often assumed by adults without research, and without checking with children themselves. This includes the view that respecting rights leads automatically to personal benefit – but this assumes that adult versions of consultation are perceived by children as their rights being respected. We know that a wide variety of actions can come under the auspices of consultation and participation – and that how they are perceived by the recipient cannot be assumed. Some consultation can look more like obtaining confirmatory views to rubber-stamp adult decisions, rather than an openness to change as a result of children/young people's perspectives.

Table 2.1 Advantages to pupils – in terms of social capital – from enhanced participation (from Hayes, 2002)

Domain	Description
Empowerment	Pupils are involved in making choices about their own learning and are involved in decisions and choices about the wider social environment that affects them.
Participation	Pupils participate fully in the learning and social activities in school.
Associational activity and common purpose	Pupils co-operate with each other in both formal and informal groups.
Supporting networks and reciprocity	Pupils support one another for either mutual or one-sided gain. There is an expectation that help would be given or received from others when needed.
Collective norms and values	Pupils and staff share common values and norms for behaviour.
Trust	Pupils trust one another and the staff and support agencies who work with them.
Safety	Pupils feel safe in school and do not restrict their use of parts of the school or aspects of school life because of fear.
Belonging	Pupils feel connected and have a sense of belonging to the school.

Professionals may perceive benefits of consultation to be the delivery of a more effective service, one leading to enhanced outcomes. Other adult-perceived benefits may be that children and young people will feel more motivated to co-operate with a service if they are involved, and more motivated to go along with the outcome. It may be that the service will be more effectively organised around child needs if children are consulted (Kirby *et al.*, 2003a). Research has found professional reports of improved service development, improved client support, increased access and use of services, and increased participatory practice (Kirby *et al.*, 2003a; Kirby *et al.*, 2003b; Sloper and Lightfoot, 2002). Critical understanding about professional practice can become apparent through consultation with children and young people – and the author hopes to demonstrate this in Chapter 3, from research findings reporting perspectives of children/young people. Benefits to children, as perceived by staff, have been: an increase in young people's sense of citizenship and social inclusion; an enhancement of their personal development (Kirby *et al.*, 2003b); and enhanced confidence and the opportunity to express ideas and feelings (Sloper and Lightfoot, 2002). Such assumed benefits may well be accurate, but would be worth verifying with children and young people themselves. Benefits to staff have been found, from staff reports, to be the realisation that children's views are important and differ from adult views, and that they provide valuable and useful ideas (Sloper and Lightfoot, 2002).

What are the best methods of consultation and participation to use?

Until recently there was little knowledge of methods used to consult with children and no evaluation of them. Policies for user engagement in many major institutions have failed to give children a voice – for example health trusts have generally failed to develop separate strands for children and young people, rarely developing different approaches (Sloper and Lightfoot, 2002). However, a range of appropriate methods is now available to consult with children and young people. The little evidence that exists has shown children to be well able to comment on what they see as good participation.

A number of innovative approaches are being developed. Punch (2002) reflected on the use of a range of different approaches to interview young people about their problems and coping strategies. The techniques included: group and individual interview; grouping and ranking exercises; spider diagrams and charts; the use of problem pages, video clips and common phrases as stimuli for discussion; and the use of a 'secret box' within which to place anonymous responses. The organisation Investing in Children, based in Durham, works in a number of ways, but commonly works with children and young people in research teams facilitated by other young people and adults (see Chapter 7). There is growing interest in the documentation of particular strategies to use with young children (Clark *et al.*, 2003; Clark and Moss, 2001). 'The mosaic approach' (Clark and Moss, 2001) recommends the use of a rich variety of data to be combined to form a living picture of what life is like for young children in a particular place – in this case a nursery school. Morris has provided, with support and advice from children with such impairments, detailed advice on ways to consult with children who have severe communication impairments (Morris, 2002).

Sloper and Lightfoot (Lightfoot and Sloper, 2003b; Sloper and

Lightfoot, 2002) have surveyed the range of methods being used, drawing on twenty-four initiatives involving young people within hospital-based health services:

- 19 initiatives used more than one method.
- 14 provided support for children such as transport, payment or training.
- 23 initiatives used some aspect of writing.
- 30 used methods that involved a verbal response.
- 16 involved the use of visual art.

Young people, it seems, did not wish to spend a lot of time on consultation, were content to let adults make the ultimate decisions and well able to recognise that other considerations including the views of adults should be taken into account (Stafford *et al.*, 2003: 372). Children cannot be regarded as a heterogeneous group – their views varied. Different young people expressed preferences for different techniques (Punch, 2002). Confidentiality was import-ant, as was being able to easily express views, and it was also important that the experience was enjoyable (Punch, 2002). Young people did not need to receive pay unless there was an ongoing involvement in consultation. Being given a meal or some activity was just as good.

Children wanted to be consulted about the area to be considered, and this seemed to be particularly important to the way Investing in Children views participation. In research that tried to access the con-cerns of young people, 200 children and young people from 3 to 18 years across Scotland wanted to be consulted about education condi-tions in school, leisure provision, public transport, health education and advice (Stafford *et al.*, 2003). Others wanted to be consulted about building clubs and leisure centres, placements if fostered and adopted, family decisions such as where to live, health decisions such as choosing your own doctor, choosing lessons to attend at school, and government decisions (Tolley *et al.*, 1998).

Interest in inclusivity was the root of a lack of enthusiasm about one-off events or youth councils, although older young people have found these of benefit. Small-group discussion was popular as being quick and convenient, but could leave out some people's views. Pro-longed group-work gave young people the opportunity to have fun, make friends and work as a team – but these could get stuck. Ques-tionnaires were approved of as enabling a larger number of children to take part, but were seen as boring, less reliable than group discussion and might not be understood by all children. Liking the questioner was important, as was an informal conversational style. It was important that there be no right or wrong answers. The language used by those consulting with children was seen to be very important – that people should avoid jargon and use vocabulary that young people themselves would use.

> parents and professionals wishing to discuss mental health with young people should either use alternative vocabulary based on young people's own, or be very careful to identify what they mean.
>
> (Armstrong *et al.*, 2000: 69)

Young people were very much aware that it would be difficult if they knew the person asking them for their views: 'you've got to spend the rest of the year with them and you might think that they might think about you and that you're like nothing' (Roose and John, 2003).

If the young person knew and liked the staff questioner this could inhibit negative comments, for fear of giving offence or getting staff into some sort of trouble. Young people advised staff to consider a questioner from another department or from outside the organisation (Lightfoot and Sloper, 2003a). This has particular implications for the evaluation of school activities and services that rarely seem to be acknowledged in published evaluations carried out by the agencies themselves with their own client group. It suggests schools and services should use an external person/body to carry out any evaluations of pupil/child service user views.

Children and young people say the following, in research, about consultation and participation

- They want to be consulted – and have things to say on any-thing that concerns them.
- Many decisions concern children and young people, and they feel they have a right to be involved.
- Consultation must lead to some real changes.
- They want to be able to set agendas for consultation – to have a say about the areas looked at and the questions asked.
- They are realistic (sometimes! often!) about the kinds of changes that are possible.

- The adults doing the consulting or leading the participation must be skilled in using approaches that help children and young people to be able to take part – these will be interesting, challenging, clear and based on values of respect and openness.
- Systems should be in place that makes it possible for them to get involved easily. This includes transport, money, refreshments and using technology in a friendly way.
- Children and young people need to be helped to develop the capacity to act effectively in debating issues with service providers. They may need time to conduct research.
- A range of young people should be included – those involved should be from a wide range of all kinds of groups of children and young people. Much younger children, disabled children and those from different ethnic heritage groups should be enabled to participate.
- Many adults would be surprised at what kinds of consultation with children and young people is possible – but only if the adults use their skills to the fullest to find the best ways to involve them!

(Cairns, 2001; Morris, 2002; Punch, 2002; Roose and John, 2003; Stafford *et al.*, 2003; Tolley *et al.*, 1998)

What are the key issues?

Consultation vs. participation?

Throughout this chapter different kinds of child involvement have been referred to. Within the research literature there have been attempts to define different kinds of participation. The most quoted is that of Hart (1992), where rungs on the ladder represent levels of participation, as follows (starting with the lowest rung): manipulation; decoration; tokenism; assigned but informed; consulted and informed; adult-initiated, shared decisions with children; child-initiated and -directed; and child-initiated, shared decisions with adults. The ladder goes from non-participation to the situation where children have the ideas, set up the project and come to adults for advice, discussion and support. This model has been critiqued as presenting an unhelpful hierarchy (Hobbs, 2005; Kirby *et al.*, 2003b) that discouragingly finds most practitioners on the lower rungs. Some suggest the use of pathways to participation, with the idea that the objective is not always to reach the top, as different degrees of power sharing can be argued to be appropriate for different situations (Kirby *et al.*, 2003b). Some criticise Hart's model for its failure to encompass a theoretical perspective that informs how to think about and go about developing pupil participation (Hobbs, 2005).

Kirby *et al.* (2003a, 2003b) have identified three different cultures of participation in organisations, those that are consultation focused, participation focused and child/youth focused (based on Shier, 2001). Kirby *et al.* suggest that certain kinds of participatory levels might be more appropriate for different organisations, depending upon 'how much they work with young people, the nature of their service and the underlying values and aims of the service' (Kirby *et al.*, 2003a: 16). The three cultures are shown in Figure 2.1.

A clear distinction arises here between consultation and participation:

• Consultation seems to involve seeking advice or information.

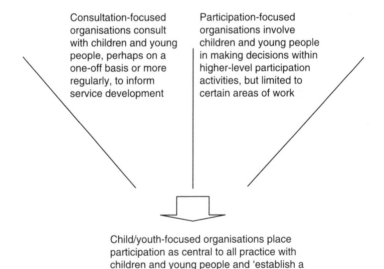

Figure 2.1 Three cultures of participation.

Adapted from Kirby *et al.*, 2003a: 16; 2003b.

- Participation seems to be about taking part and sharing in something.

Much of the current increase in activity has been more about seeking the views of children and young people than a sharing of some kind of development or decision-making with them. It is hard to imagine that the kind of partnership needed for inclusive education would not require the sharing of decision-making.

It's difficult

Involving children and young people is not necessarily straightforward and effortless. Benefits do not necessarily come easily, and the false starts, and efforts at consultation where snags have encountered tend not to be reported. Problems have included (Sloper and Lightfoot, 2002) the difficulties in getting young people involved, the difficulties in getting adults to take young people's views seriously, trying to please everyone, making sure everyone's views were heard, and dealing with unrealistic expectations that might result from consultation. The time needed can also be a problem. Some organisations seem better placed to engage young people in participatory processes and events. Levels of activity vary across institutions. For some organisations a policy without action seemed to be the main approach (Cutler and Taylor, 2003). Surveys have found that most organisations seemed to want assistance in how to go about child involvement in order to 'work their way through a challenging and unfamiliar process' (Cutler and Taylor, 2003: 107). Some key observations about gaps and issues:

- There are not many children and young people routinely, as part of the culture of everyday life in schools and services, being consulted or playing a more participatory role.
- There is in no sense a major 'child voice' in the development of local or national policy – and little beyond tokenism in any examples of the involvement of children and young people in major local authority reorganisations.
- The voices of certain children/young people are heard and not others (returned to in the following section).
- There seems to be more participation in public decision-making than in private decision-making, in the process of using schools and services (considered more comprehensively in Chapter 3).

- Organisations in the voluntary sector seem to be better placed than public agencies to engage young people in participation.
- And, related to this perhaps, practitioners/professionals/workers may not be in the best position to ask their own clients what they think of services – however skilled they are in interpersonal relationships. Evaluation might best be carried out by young people themselves facilitated by an external body.

One option for organisations is to gain expertise from external sources or go into partnership with another agency where there is experience in consulting with children. Consultation and other kinds of involvement may need to be seen as a multi-layered process – to develop organisational enthusiasm – and not to be consigned to one-off events. Organisations may consider becoming listening institutions, where consultation is integrated into all activities in an appropriate manner, and is always developing. This may require a number of changes, including the designation of a lead official with time and resources located in the most relevant section, a senior-level 'champion' at board level with real commitment (Kirby *et al.*, 2003a; Kirby *et al.*, 2003b).

Some are consulted more than others

There are also problems in the level of inclusivity of children who have access to participatory actions. Certain groups of young people seem to be consulted with and involved in participation activities less than others. The most common age range for the agencies from Kirby *et al.*'s database sample to work with was 12 to 16, but all ages were included in the participatory work, with many projects working across a range of age groups (Kirby *et al.*, 2003b: 36). There is evidence (Fundudis, 2003) of thinking in some services that age, and professional assessment of such things as maturity and ability, is a clear limiting factor on the degree of consultation possible. However, other researchers and practitioners stress the need for consultation with the very young and can give examples and provide methods (Clark *et al.*, 2003; Clark and Moss, 2001). Similarly, consultation with children with disabilities was far less in evidence than with children without disabilities (Kirby *et al.*, 2003b). However, Morris's guidelines on how to consult with children with severe communication disabilities (Morris, 2002) developed with children with communication disabilities is a challenge to find ways to involve and include all children and young people whatever the level of disability:

Never believe it if someone says to you 'he can't communicate' or 'its impossible to find out his views or feelings'. Always start from the assumption that a young person is at least capable of expressing a preference. Everyone expresses preferences – likes, dislikes, happiness, discomfort. If you can recognise how someone expresses a preference, or a dislike, you are receiving a message from them. That is communication and it can lead to the young person having choice and control in their lives . . .

(Morris, 2002)

Many suggest that an appropriative range of approaches need to be developed that do not always focus just on written and verbal responses, and find appropriate approaches for children using alternative communication methods. Children need to have some say in both the method of consultation or participation and the scope or topics.

Children and young people, when asked, are vociferous in their view that the process of consultation should be open and inclusive (Cairns, 2001; Lightfoot and Sloper, 2003a; Stafford *et al.*, 2003; Tolley *et al.*, 1998). One group of young people in an NCB (National Children's Bureau) research project looking at consultation found children thought certain groups of children were missed out when it came to having a say. This included teenagers, younger children, disabled children, and young people with problems such as drugs (Tolley *et al.*, 1998). A child involved in a participation project said:

So that big people can see things from a little kid's eyes. 'Cos little kids can see what big people may not realise. Like the story of the Emperor's New Clothes, when the Emperor was walking naked and it was only a little kid that saw that the emperor was walking naked. Little kids see things that big people may not realise and that's why I think that little kids should have a say as well.

(Tolley *et al.*, 1998: 1)

Participation should be inclusive and highly sensitive to the need to give voice to and have involvement with young people from groups less well represented in current consultations and participatory processes. Children/young people also want to be consulted in ways that recognise their universality as children rather than to consider them as different. There is a need to find ways to listen to all voices and recognise the diversity of perspectives.

Ideas about childhood constrain participation

Cultural assumptions about what children are and how adults should be in relationship to them play a significant part in how easy it is for practitioners to work collaboratively with them. If children are regarded as 'innocents to be protected' or 'wild beasts to be tamed' – or 'objects of scrutiny to be examined' before providing professional treatments – there is little room for partnership. We are faced with a contradictory array of understandings about childhood: many, but not all, more consistent with relationships that run counter to collaboration.

Consistent *with* participation is a rights agenda for children. The 1989 United Nations Convention on the Rights of the Child stated in Article 12 that all children should have the opportunity to express views in processes affecting them. Children's views were to be considered according to age and maturity.

The role of psychology in the development of models of childhood has been powerful and contradictory. Child-centred psychology (i.e. Piaget, Bruner) drew attention to the child as an active learner and started to change the relationship between the learner and the teacher. This thinking has been taken further by Vygotskian psychology, focusing on the reciprocity of the relationship between children and adults. This psychology has informed an understanding of the agency of children/young people in learning and development, and (therefore) in shaping the actions of teachers and carers. Alternatively, other strands of psychology (psychometrics, cognitive psychology) define child actions in terms of abilities and social competencies that can be measured, some of which are relatively fixed. This essentialist and structuralist thinking leads to adult judgements, sometimes with a call for assessments, of a child's maturity and skills (Fundudis, 2003). Such an approach more often puts limits on the degree of consultation with children, and puts any decision about how and when to consult firmly in the hands of adults, and generally not any adults, but those deemed professionally qualified to make such a judgement.

The prime effect of child abuse scandals from the 1970s onwards was a call for more effective delivery and co-ordination of services. The consequences of these scandals have been in general to give agency more to the state, and less to the family or to the child (Wyness, 2000: 4). However, in contrast, the development of protective systems 'establish[ed] the formative position of children as legal and moral subjects' (Wyness, 2000: 4) and inquiry reports led to a less voluble call for services to listen to children. Dame Butler-Sloss, in the report of the inquiry into the Cleveland scandal, found that: 'The views and wishes of the child, particularly as to what should happen to him/her, should be taken into account by the professionals involved with their problems' (HMSO, 1988: 245). This inquiry led in the large part to the Children Act 1989 in England and 1990 in Scotland, which imposed a statutory duty on those responsible for identifying children's needs to take account of the ascertainable wishes and feelings of the child in care proceedings.

The Children Act started a quiet revolution as the need to consult with children, even in a prescribed area, was now on the agenda, but much subsequent legislation made no mention of the need to consult with children. However, professional groups held conferences on children's perspectives (Gibbs and Stoker, 1996), practical tools were published to involve children in assessment and reviews (Gersch *et al.*, 1993; Davie and Galloway, 1995), and there was a steady increase in related research (Cooper, 1993; Cooper and McIntyre, 1995; Blatchford, 1996a; Blatchford, 1996b; Rudduck and Chaplain, 1995). The revolution was indeed quiet. Changes in practices in services to consult with children were limited. Furthermore, calls to listen to children were also accompanied by renewed reminders of other discourses that tell of limited ability of children to give authentic views (Fundudis, 2003; Walker *et al.*, 1991).

Whilst consulting children and young people is a fairly clearly noted aspiration of much of public policy, a much more powerfully experienced change in children's lives over the last 50 years has been that their lives have become more and more prescribed by adults, in the form of the family, school and the state. Opportunities for children to define use of their own time within spaces not surveilled by adults have become rare. Children's school experience has become more and more controlled by the state, whether through national curriculum or through Ofsted's school inspections. Children have become units of assessment and achievement, with real implications for schools, as a result of their SATs and GCSE scores. With more leisure, sports, arts and music facilities and with more after-school provision at school, leisure time for many children has become more and more organised, and often an extension of school.

Conclusion

Kirby *et al.* (2003a: 17) in the DfES-funded handbook about how to go about involving children and young people, states that if an organisation works regularly and directly with children and young people ... such organisations should aim to be child/youth focused ... so that children and young people's views and experiences [can] influence decisions about their personal care as well as input into public decisions about how services are delivered to them as a group.

This would presumably include *all* schools and *all* other agencies working directly with children – such as health professionals, educational professionals and those in social services and voluntary agencies. We have a long way to go. The key change that is required is a shift from consultation – from asking children their views. Where we need to go is towards more authentic participation – towards the sharing with children and young people in the development of schools and services and their involvement in decisions taken about them in education, health and social care. In some areas we have succeeded in resisting certain understandings of childhood (i.e. a child is to be protected, a child does not have skills to articulate robust views) whose stories call us into objectifying children and subjugating them within professional processes. The evidence for such resistance is the massive increase in activity to consult with children over policy and research, and, in a few organisations, to involve children fully. However, further moves from consultation into more participative practice is likely to involve the development in professionals of greater political literacy about the implications of narrow structuralist conclusions of childhood, and the ways they are supported by other discourses, including those that constitute how we see the professional role. Flesh is put on the bones of these ideas in the following chapters, with further elaboration in Chapter 6, and examples of practice in Chapter 7. The Appendix lists, on the basis of research, suggested qualities that children and young people might want in the services they use.

3   The absent special guest
Children as service users

I wouldn't say anything personal [to my doctor] because he's my dad's friend.

They [social workers] see you as like more dangerous than you are, man, sometimes.

They [teachers] don't get to know you enough because there are so many of you.

We don't really get a say – we just do as we're told.

It affects us and all. It don't affect adults. It affects kids more than it does adults.

(Tolley *et al.*, 1998: 10, 19, 25)

Don't just provide information for young people – spend more time talking to them to help them understand what is happening.

(Lingard, 2002: 5)

Introduction

Children's participation in personal decision-making requires knowledge, understanding, choice and control in their use of services to do with health, educational, welfare, leisure and legal issues. Such participation is key to the relationship between children and inclusive education. These services play important roles in different ways in a young person's inclusion or exclusion from education. Statutory agencies often try to facilitate inclusion and other services assist in more indirect ways in the general relationship between a young person and society, in whether the young person is socially included or excluded from the main institutions of society. It is difficult to see how there can be any participation in inclusive education without participation in personal decision-making, without child involvement in the services they interact with as users. The review in Chapter 2 of the current

situation of child participation found that an increase in the consultation of children and young people in some areas of more public
decision-making does not seem to have been matched by more participation in schools and in the services children use. There are certainly
developments in this area – but also major gaps and problems. Just
what is the situation and what further changes are possible? What
actions are open to professionals who want to engage in more
collaborative relationships with children and young people? After
looking at the policy context, this chapter considers the following
questions:

- To what extent do professionals involve children and young
  people?
- What do children and young people make of the services they
  use? What do children know about professional roles? How do
  children experience professional involvement?
- Why does it seem to be so difficult for professionals to involve
  children and young people in decision-making?

Policy context

It is worth being reminded of the strong political and legislative context for listening to children and involving them in decision-making:
the 1989 UN Convention of Rights of Child, the 1989 Children Act,
the 1990 Children Act Scotland, the Code of Practice on Special Needs
(DfES, 2001a; DfES, 2001b), the Education Act 2002, and the
National Service Framework for Children, Young People and Maternity Services (DH and DfES, 2004). The 'every child matters' agenda
places the emphasis more on 'consultation' than on 'participation' –
more on involving children and young people in the 'planning, delivery
and evaluation of policies and services' (HMSO, 2003: 83) than on
their involvement in service use and decision-making at a personal
level. However, other current legislation and policy very much endorse
involvement at a personal level. The following quotes give a flavour of
these intentions:

> provide the best and most exciting opportunities we can to allow
> children and young people to get involved and get active.
>
> (Scottish Executive, 2003: 31)

> At all stages of decision making children's views should be taken
> seriously. . . .

No assumptions should be made about categories of children with disabilities who cannot share in decision making or give consent before examination, assessment or treatment.

(Children Act, 1989: 27)

All children should be involved in making decisions where possible right from the start of their education . . . Participation in education is a process that will necessitate all children being given the opportunity to make choices and understand that their views matter.

(Code of Practice on Special Needs, para 3.6;
DfES, 2001a; DfES, 2001b)

Every child, young person and parent is actively involved in decisions about the child's health and well-being, based on appropriate information.

(National Service Framework for Children, Young People and
Maternity Services: 89; DH and DfES, 2004)

What do professionals need to do to make their interactions with children and young people more participative? Evidence of collaborative relationships between professionals and children is considered before looking at what children say about the services they use.

To what extent do professionals involve children and young people?

It is very difficult to get an accurate picture about the extent to which professionals make efforts to listen to children and involve them in decision-making. There is very little research on professional actions and attitudes in this area. The research presented in this section will focus more on one particular professional, educational psychologists (EPs), than others, as a result of the author's support of research on participation within this particular professional group. The author is an educational psychologist involved in supporting small-scale research carried out by EPs and EPs in training as part of post-graduate degrees. Personal communication – and research – suggests that other professionals have similar approaches to consultation, and where this is available it will be referred to.

An accurate picture might include the views of professionals on whether, when and how to involve children, and the factors that constitute their views. It might also include details about how professionals enable children and young people to be in the position where they understand the role of the person they are seeing, and are able to take part in decision-making. The research carried out by Galloway *et al.* (1994) and Armstrong (1995) found many, but not all, EPs tried to explain their role. However, there is little research into how this actually happens. Grossman (2005) found four of the five EPs interviewed, from different LEAs, rarely consulted children as they saw this as someone else's responsibility or felt the professional role was to act in the child's best interests. Part of this involved a failure to explain their role:

> We do leave it up to the school really. I suppose because they have filled in that [referral] form we expect them to have talked through what it's for.
>
> I usually ask parents to let the children know when I'm coming and who I am.

There is very little research into how professionals explain their role to children – and what messages about involvement are conveyed. Exceptions are Hobbs (2000) and Clarke (2006) who asked (respectively) 35 and 58 EPs to tell them how they introduced themselves to children. At first sight the introductions seemed informative. Hobbs found most EPs gave their name, identified themselves as an EP, described what an EP did, established whether the child/young person had expected the meeting and knew who they were and why they were meeting, checked it was OK to continue with the meeting, and explained what would happen in the meeting. Clarke found only three responses explained what an EP was and described their role and the purpose of meeting with any explicitness. Hobbs (2000) similarly found a lack of lucidity in explanations given. She suggests it is the attempt to reduce the lack of normality in the situation that leads to the ambiguity about the EP role. Little helpful information was conveyed and instead the message was likely to confuse rather than inform. For example, the presence of an EP was an unusual event, and yet EPs often used phrases to claim otherwise (Hobbs, 2000): 'I visit your school every month to see different children . . . did your mum say someone was coming in . . . your teacher told me . . . I used to be a teacher . . . We deal with problems lots of people have or find themselves in all the time' (adapted from several responses). The reference to the child's parent and teacher could raise confidentiality issues for the child, and make it difficult for the child or young person to know how any information they gave to the EP might be dealt with. The reference to 'problems' is general, gives no idea what problems are being suggested, and focuses on deficits. By implication, some discussions have already happened about the child to which the child has not been party.

Kirby *et al.*'s (2003b) research found an informal approach was quite often used to gain children's views, especially those of younger children. It seems that instead of asking, the approach taken was to informally spending time 'being with' (Kirby *et al.*, 2003b) children – engaging in joint activities, listening, observing child-initiated dialogue and informal conversation. Whilst there is much to be gained from finding ways to talk to children that communicate with them on their own terms and through their own interests, there are clear dangers here that adults might make inaccurate assumptions about how the world looks for a child, about the child's needs and perspectives, and that these may not represent the perspectives of the child.

A range of reasons were given from research for not consulting children and not involving them in meetings and decisions. These come from a range of professional groups:

- Age was the most common reason given, and this was related to a 'lack of children's skills for communication' and 'understanding of the situation'. This reason was given in small-scale research with a number of different professionals: educational psychologists (Grossman, 2005), co-ordinators of family group conferences (Hughes, 2002), teachers who are special needs co-ordinators (SENCOs), social workers and non-social workers involved in child protection conferences (Shemmings, 2000), social workers involved in meetings with looked after children (Thomas and O'Kane, 1999), and medical practitioners (Dixon-Woods *et al.*, 1999; Fundudis, 2003; Geller *et al.*, 2003; Simmons, 2003).
- The demands of the situation was another reason, i.e. that as family group conferences were not aimed to be a therapeutic process but to provide an alternative decision-making process, it was not appropriate to talk to the child before the family group conference as it was up to the family as to how they manage decision-making (Hughes, 2002).
- Parents speaking for the child constituted another barrier – observed by SENCOs in school meetings (Caine, 2001) and medical practitioners (Tates and Meeuwesen, 2001; Young *et al.*, 2006).
- Lack of professional skills, and the need for training in this area was acknowledged by medical professionals (Hart and Chesson, 1998), and co-ordinators of family group conferences (Hughes, 2002). Uncertainty about how to manage shared decision-making

was mentioned in medical contexts (Dixon-Woods *et al.*, 1999; Gabe *et al.*, 2004).

- Evidence that consulting children leads to good outcomes for children was requested by medical practitioners (Dixon-Woods *et al.*, 1999).
- The need to protect the child from the responsibility of decisions (Grossman, 2005; Sandbaek, 1999), or from growing up too fast (Shemmings, 2000) were common professional beliefs.

Grossman (2005) gives examples of rationalisations for not involving children. Four EPs (out of five interviewed) who did not see consulting children as part of their role referred to a feeling that the child's view would not change matters but also a sense that it was the EP's role to take responsibility, plus the recurring theme of age as an essential consideration:

> I didn't want to put him through it again to be honest because he has got so much on his plate really and he had had all that assessment from psychiatrists as well and I just thought one more person poking around when I don't really need to do it then there's just no need for it really.
>
> I just find that a lot of schools presume that it's about what the professionals think, what the adults think ... that the pupil's views is not going to change things anyway.
>
> If he was older, maybe he would have been more [involved] ...
>
> It just felt like ... as adults we go in and act on children's best interest, and it just felt that ... was she there, no, why, we were acting on her best interest ... I do strongly believe that they should be involved but it's a very fine line.
>
> Upon reflection, I suppose I should have really consulted him about the kind of school that he would like to go to or whether was still happy where he was.

However, a more optimistic picture is presented by Thomas and O'Kane's (1999) survey of 225 looked after children aged 8 to 12 in the late 1990s of participation with social workers in decision-making processes. They suggest that the proportion of children who had been invited to take part in reviews and planning meetings, estimated at between half and two-thirds of the sample, was far more than in the past. Age remained a consideration – for children under 10 the proportion was lower. Children were less likely to be involved in meetings if 'big' decisions had to be made or if there was conflict between the local authority and their families. The social workers felt that in 87 per cent of cases children's views were genuinely listened to, and that this did not vary with their age or with their presence at meetings. Such a view is confirmed by other research looking at social workers working with children in a child-protection context (Shemmings, 2000). Similarly, encouraging case studies demonstrating young people's participation in regeneration initiatives are documented by the Neighbourhood Renewal Unit (2006). In research in a school context, of twenty SENCOs, nineteen said children were invited to attend meetings and always needed some preparation, fifteen reported that pupil views were always represented in meetings and six that pupils were debriefed after the meetings. All respondents were SENCOs at middle, second-ary and special schools and all children were aged 9 and over (Caine, 2001). Researchers in a medical context drew attention to the need to think very much of involving the parent(s) with the child or young person (Tates and Meeuwesen, 2001; Gabe *et al.*, 2004).

From the DfES survey of participation, there is evidence that in a small range of contexts children may be being supported in making personal decisions (Kirby *et al.*, 2003b). These decisions involved chil-dren/young people in consent about participation, choice of play and leisure activities, and decisions about their own learning, health treat-ment and care support. Case studies from the DfES survey showed a Family Group Conference Project that enabled children to make self-referrals. This allowed children to decide whether this type of approach, the Family Group Conference, would be helpful to them. Kirby *et al.* (2003b) found less activity in primary health organisations in this area than in educational and social services. There were, how-ever, signs of much interest from services in finding ways to develop more collaborative ways of working with children. This is evidenced by the increasing number of organisations requesting research carried out by young people to find out what kind of services young people want ('Investing in Children' website http://www.durham.gov.uk/iic and personal report).

Where children and young people are actively involved by profes-sionals, the rationale is likely to include a reference to a child's rights to be included, reference to their capabilities, and acknowledgement of the need for professionals to be skilled in communicating appropri-ately with children. Children and young people from a variety of ages, ethnic heritages, disabilities, special needs, or exclusion from school have been found to be well able to comment on their needs and on the services they experience (Madge and Fassam, 1982; Allen, 1999; Burke and Grosvenor, 2003; Lightfoot and Sloper, 2003a; Tolley *et al.*,

1998; Morris, 2002; Gimrax and Bell, 2004; Barnett *et al.*, 2005). Health professionals are urged to be inclusive in the National Service Framework for Children (2004: 90): 'children and young people who are often excluded from participation activities are supported in giving their views e.g. disabled or looked after children'.

There is an increasing call for professionals to use appropriate approaches (Hart and Chesson, 1998) to 'communicate directly with children and young people, attempting to see the world through their eyes, using the child's preferred communication method or language' (DH and DfES, 2004: 90). To counter the idea that children and young people lack skills, Kirby (2003) suggests young people develop their skills through actually participating in decision-making. The responsibility is therefore placed with professionals.

There is a growing range of high quality tools to support professionals in collaborative practice that have been advanced by voluntary organisations including Scope and Save the Children. A group of educational psychologists have set in motion a variety of possible materials to use to communicate with a child at different times in the association of a professional in the educational life of a child (Hobbs *et al.*, 2000; Todd, 2000b; Todd, 2003b; Todd, 2003c). Trainee EPs at Newcastle University have evolved much practice in consulting with children and a group of EPs have produced a CD containing materials to adapt for use in different contexts (Cassavella *et al.*, 2002). These have included:

- a story-board with pictures of professionals talking to children, to assist a conversation with a child about what working with a professional might involve;
- fold-up leaflets explaining who the educational psychologist is;
- letters inviting a child to a meeting and suggesting what it might be about;
- letters summarising a meeting with a child; and
- reports for the child and written with the child.

Simkins (2001) reports on the response of six children to the use of letters to them as a part of educational psychology input with the children. The letters were written using ways of thinking sympathetic to narrative and solution-focused practices (see Chapter 7). Children said the letters seemed to clarify for them the purpose and aims of consultations. Their responses were positive: 'it made me feel important, that someone was listening'; 'never had letters before'; 'I was pleased because it was positive (and letters home are usually negative)'.

There are some excellent examples of the 'how to' variety together with a range of creative tools – all for professionals to use to negotiate what happens when a child and a professional meet. There are also some indications that children may be becoming more involved in decision-making. However, there are also strong indications that professionals have a well-defended and enduring wall of reasons not to collaborate. These will be returned to again at the end of this chapter (and also in Chapter 6) after looking at the perspectives of children and young people.

What children and young people make of the services they use

'They had a funny name I cannot pronounce' – what children know about the professional's role

There is now a growing research literature on the perspectives of children and young people on the roles of professionals, some of this research carried out by young people themselves (Gimrax and Bell, 2004; Barnett *et al.*, 2005; Tolley *et al.*, 1998). There is no shortage of ideas from children and young people about the services they might want, and what we know about this from some of the research available is summarised in the Appendix. The main finding from research, considering the question of what children make of current services, is a lack of knowledge on the part of children and young people of the roles of professionals they have been asked to see. A wide range of professionals are referred to in the research, including CAMHS workers, social workers, educational psychologists and doctors.

There is some evidence that knowledge of different professional roles is not accurately available to children and young people. Therefore, prior to being asked to see a professional, there is every likelihood that they will have an unclear and ambiguous understanding of the role of the person they are being asked to see. For example, Lingard (2002) asked thirty young people who were attending a youth club what they thought was the role of educational psychologists. Any involvement the young people had with professionals was not known. Twelve thought EPs gave general help with difficulty in school, six thought they gave specific help in school (i.e. for children who are dyslexic, or supporting people with behaviour difficulties), four spoke of general helping without mentioning school, four thought they gave help related to mental health issues ('works with psychos', 'can read your mind', 'helps people with mental problems'), and six had other ideas entirely ('works with footballers that hurt themselves', 'teaches people about computers', and 'the CID police'). About half, therefore, did not have any factually based idea of the role of the EP. As EPs vary considerably in how they see their own responsibilities, some EPs might even reject many of the ideas expressed by the young people, bringing the number of inaccurate beliefs even higher. Looking at a different service, that of counselling offered by two full-service extended schools in the UK, Tiplady (2005) asked children who did not see the school-based counsellor what they thought was being offered. She found they had little understanding of the role, why they would see one or how they would arrange a meeting.

A group of young people researched a CAMHS service in the North of England for the human rights organisation that is part of Durham County Council. The young people were also service users and answered a question about what they had believed about CAMHS prior to seeing a worker. This question attracted the following responses: 'Its about Skitzo's'; 'Help you cope with life'; 'Thick people go there' (Barnett *et al.*, 2005).

The CAMHS research also raises questions about the level of information given to young people to enable choice over whether to access a service. Of the fourteen young people researchers, only one had ever been asked if they wanted to be referred to the CAMHS service (Gimrax and Bell, 2004). The others had been referred without any discussion with them or their consent. Young people who were seeing CAMHS workers often did not know workers were part of CAMHS or what CAMHS was. One asked for information from a youth offending supervisor and was told to find out for themselves (Gimrax and Bell, 2004). Prior to attending a school counselling service, the most frequent view of young people who were asked to consider taking this service (of thirteen respondents to a questionnaire) was that they felt 'scared', 'happy', 'relieved' and 'unsure' (Tiplady, 2005).

Even when children and young people have met different professionals and are receiving a service from them, their level of knowledge about the role of the person they are seeing seems to remain at a low level. The most extensive and detailed research, an ESRC-funded project, was carried out by Galloway *et al.* (1994) and Armstrong (1995) involving 47 children. Seven were attending an off-site special unit for primary aged children with behaviour difficulties, eleven were attending two residential schools for EBD and twenty-nine were currently undergoing a statutory assessment for behaviour. Children, parents and professionals were interviewed over a period of time during the process of statutory assessment of their special educational needs, and some meetings were observed. Perceptions of children suggest the role of practitioners they had seen had not been communicated by professionals in an adequate manner: '[decisions were made by] my taxi lady'; '[I was seen by] a psychology teacher when I was at the hospital'; 'they had a funny name I cannot pronounce' (Galloway *et al.*, 1994).

A significant proportion of the children in contact with child welfare services and protection, school counselling or the child psychiatry clinic in a wealthy suburb in Oslo did not know why they were seeing someone (Sandbaek, 1999). Sandbaek interviewed 24 children (20 boys and 4 girls) and found that about half the children said they knew why they were seeing someone, and about a third had only a vague understanding of why they were seeing someone: 'I don't know why I have counselling. The teacher just told me to go there'; 'I was seeing a person from the Child Psychiatric Clinic because my mum and I argued a lot ... I guess I could have talked to her about difficult issues, but I never did ... I didn't like seeing her very much. I felt it was all nonsense! It may have helped a little, but not much' (1999: 113–114).

Young people find names like 'educational psychologist' (Lingard, 2002) and 'CAMHS' and terms like 'mental health' difficult (Armstrong *et al.*, 2000). 'Educational psychologist' was seen to be confusing and young people did not understand what it meant. The word 'mental' in CAMHS was felt to be too negative and 'makes you sound like a psycho', and therefore the name had a stigma (Gimrax and Bell, 2004). Young people seem to prefer words like worry, stress, or depressed to mental health.

Child views about their experience of professional involvement

When decisions are made about young people about their educational or home placement, or about some kind of intervention, be it medication, counselling, an educational programme or mentoring, there is evidence that children have not been placed in a position where they have understanding about how such decisions were reached and neither have they been situated so they can have much involvement in those decisions.

Parents whose children acted as their carers reported that at no point had their children been involved in discussion about their caring responsibilities, or their own needs, or their understanding of their parents' health and difficulties. Neither had they been informed or advised on care management issues (Aldridge and Becker, 1994).

Similar perceptions were reported by children whose parents or carers are HIV positive (Kay *et al.*, 2004). Children/young people's perspectives, exemplified in the following quotes, seem to suggest they had been left with an understanding of their educational placements (either in units attached to a school or in a special school) in broadly negative terms, as a response to poor behaviour, rather than a positive response to need (Armstrong, 1995; Galloway *et al.*, 1994):

> I don't know why I'm picked out but I think it means there's something odd about me.
> He wants to send me away. I don't know why. He hasn't told me.
> [The educational psychologist] finds a place for you to go if you've been bad of if you've no home.
> [After exclusion from school] they had to start [the assessment] because there was nowhere to go.
> I got sent here [the unit] because of my reading, not because of my behaviour ... Dyslexia means you've got a short mind and can't read so well. It's like amnesia but you forget things.
> Because I was not good enough.

Similarly, from other research:

> the children themselves expressed a lack of interest in the process which led to the placement, and almost all of them stated it had resulted from a single incident which took place in school, over which they had no control.
>
> (Farrell *et al.*, 1996)

> Don't have no say [in foster and residential care] – they just put you in a place.
>
> (Tolley *et al.*, 1998: 23)

> They don't put anything what's good about you [in secure unit reports], they just try and put all the bad things about you.
>
> (Tolley *et al.*, 1998: 19)

> You go to a special school. You must be thick (Julie).
>
> (Wise, 2000: 135)

In research carried out by young people into a CAMHS service, some young people had been given medication without knowing why they needed it or how it will benefit them (Gimrax and Bell,

2004). Side effects, which the young people found frightening, had not been explained. Ruegger (2001) similarly found children had not been enabled to fully understand the implications of the role of the Guardian ad Litem. They interviewed forty-seven children from two counties, aged between 7 and 16, eight of whom had a learning difficulty of some kind and four were from different ethnic minority groups. Children were generally positive about this service but there was one area children identified as particularly problematic. This was the area of knowledge about confidentiality, about who had access to information given by the children and young people to the Guardian. The research found that many children were shocked when the report of the Guardian ad Litem was made known not only to the judge but also to their natural parents, and also when the Guardian ad Litem expressed their own opinion in court.

A study of the perspectives of children diagnosed with ADHD and taking psychostimulants revealed that many believed ADHD to be a brain disorder and that they had little understanding of the effects and purposes of medication. They believed that the main purpose of the medication was to control behaviour, although this did not match with their daily experiences. They also had essentially negative views about themselves and generally thought that not taking the tablets was something they would welcome (Arora and Mackay, 2004).

In another study four young people who, when younger, had lived with sexual abuse spoke about their experience of professional involvement. One felt the social services procedures had been to her benefit. The other three had negative perspectives: there was a general feeling of not knowing what was going on. Their experience was of being required to provide what the professionals needed to do their job rather than being listened to and treated in ways that would help them personally (Aldridge, 2003).

However, in a study of fifteen looked-after children aged 10 to 15 (Munro, 2001) the social worker was seen as very powerful and a very strong ally when the relationship worked well. Most could remember at least one social worker with whom they had experienced support and a good relationship. The biggest concern was the high turnover of social workers. For some, review meetings were positive, and for others they left young people feeling powerless and frustrated. Of six 'vulnerable' children aged 5 to 11, two had seen an educational psychologist and had felt listened to, and wanted the social worker to tell her more about what was going on (Aubrey and Dahl, 2006). There is a similar range of comments from other research, carried out by young people themselves:

A friend has a social worker. She used to take him out everywhere, cos his parents like didn't give a damn about him.

They [youth workers] only, most of them are normally like nice and like kind to you, but it's just not enough, you know, really, not enough nice people around that really, really wanna help you, just a couple of them. Everyone else just thinks you are a kid.

Some doctors treat you like adults and others treat you like kids.

(Tolley *et al.*, 1998: 18–19)

Similarly, a focus group of eight young people who had experienced contact with an educational psychologist expressed positive views of the service. Young people felt listened to, had been given feedback and valued confidentiality (Woolfson and Harker, 2002). Ten of thirteen young people attending a school counselling service felt some kind of positive benefit (Tiplady, 2005).

The research referred to so far has suggested that children and young people see professionals without reliable information or without a process that enables them to reach a situation of unambiguously understanding the role of the professionals they are asked to see. There is evidence that this lack of understanding persists even when the delivery of the service has taken place. This is not surprising given the vagueness with which it seems professionals introduce themselves to children (Hobbs, 2000). Not only are they situated so that little understand of the role of the professional is likely to be available to them, but there is also evidence that the basis of interventions or decisions that might result from contact with a professional are not made clear to them. Once they meet with professionals, children and young people's experiences of such interactions is very mixed:

- there is a lack of understanding about how decisions were reached;
- concerns about of confidentiality;
- professionals' decisions believed by children to confirm negative characteristics or focus on blame/punishment;
- a valuing of contact with some professionals for the support provided.

Clearly there are some positive relationships between children and professionals, but there is also a worrying context of a lack of information and involvement. What might be the implications of this for the well-being of children and young people? Implications are suggested, with reference to the research by Galloway *et al.* (1994) and Armstrong (1995). This research investigated the experience over a period of time of the involvement of young people with professionals, ascertaining the views of children, parents and professionals at various times and collecting information about the outcomes of assessments.

Three examples, paraphrased from their research, are presented in cases 1, 2 and 3.

The three case studies have been paraphrased from the research, and obviously omit much detail from the original situation. However, they are the result of careful, systematic research carried out over time. What they seem to say, at the very least, is that there was a situation of mutual misunderstanding on the part of both the professionals and the young people. The young people in the examples did not seem to have been placed in a situation where they understood either the role of the educational psychologist (EP) or the purpose of the assessment. The young people nevertheless constructed their own view of the role

---

Case 1

A personality assessment of Peter by the psychologist gives the outcome that:

> he is very introverted with a high level of neuroticism and a range of features that indicate he is specifically depressed – a reduction of interest – one could almost say he showed no emotion.
>
> (Galloway *et al.*, 1994: 62)

In a discussion with the educational psychologist, the clinical medical officer said:

> he didn't display any emotion about his life. Nothing seemed to surprise him about his home and social life.
>
> (Galloway *et al.*, 1994: 62)

These observations were used by the psychologist and CMO in support of their joint recommendation that Peter would benefit from placement in a residential school for children with emotional and behavioural difficulties.

> (Galloway *et al.*, 1994: 62)

Peter's view to the researcher was that the:

> assessment threatened his chances of continuing to live with his family and as such was a considerable source of anxiety.
>
> (Galloway *et al.*, 1994: 62)

However, this was not expressed to any of the professionals. According to the researchers, the professionals saw a lack of response and this reinforced their assessment of him. The researchers conclude that anxiety about the assessment process, expressed by Peter as a lack of response, was taken by the professional to denote some kind of internal pathology requiring residential placement (paraphrased from Galloway *et al.*, 1994).

Case 2

A psychologist gave Darren an opportunity to make his views known, but Darren believed the assessment was taking place because his teachers were saying 'I was the worst 1st in the year'. He expressed his own account to the researcher:

> There were a lot of people aggravating me because I wasn't very bright. I was more or less the thickest kid in the class and I used to smash out at them . . . I got on with the teachers bad. They just didn't know what my problems were . . . I used to always get taken the rip out of and that was the trouble really. I never bothered to listen. I just sat there making jokes.
>
> (Galloway *et al.*, 1994: 60)

The researchers report that Darren did not feel able to give his side of the story:

> There was nothing I could say really because they wouldn't have me back in school . . . I didn't want to be away from my family and friends but he [the psychologist] put me here [residential school]. He's the one who got me sent away.
>
> (Galloway *et al.*, 1994: 60)

Case 3

David, aged 12, seemed to interpret 'statementing' as the same as 'sectioning' and believed he would be admitted to a mental hospital, which was consistent with the view of David's parents who maintained there was 'something wrong in the head'. The researchers saw no evidence of an explanation given to the parents or to David of the purpose of the assessment, and they suggested David's misunderstanding of the assessment impeded his ability to give his perspective on his situation. In the view of the researchers, this led to a lack of consideration in the assessment of David's concerns about family relationships:

> by focusing attention upon David rather than upon the relationships within his family, the assessment, unintentionally, added to the problems David was encountering. The lack of information available to him impeded his ability to make sense of the assessment other than in terms of his own personal deficit. Yet, because this was his understanding of the purpose of the assessment, he was unable to contribute anything to it.
>
> (Galloway *et al.*, 1994: 61)

---

of the EP, and in all cases this view meant that they were not in a position where they could put forward their own perspectives about their own situation. In none of the cases did it appear that the views of the young person were available to the EP, and in one of the cases a lack of response from the young person was articulated in pathological terms. Potentially very serious consequences for the lives of the young people are suggested by the researchers as a result of this lack of communication.

Conclusion: why does it seem to be so difficult for professionals to involve children and young people in decision-making?

Children/young people who see professionals for help often seem to be the *absent special guest*. They seem to be called into existence, like a genie, by everyone except themselves. It is as if the vision of the genie that has appeared, as a result of practitioners rubbing the lamp, is actually a grey imitation of the exciting picture of the real technicolour person. The practitioners do not realise the riches that could be available, and the child, the genie, does not know how to get out of the lamp.

Professionals try to do the best they can, often under quite stressful circumstances, to exercise their role according to what they understand as good practice. Professional practice is powerfully shaped by a range of different understandings for what 'doing one's best' in relationships with children might mean. A discourse of protecting children and taking adult responsibility to solve children's problems, and finding children's views where appropriate can be contrasted with a discourse of rights. The latter assumes the use of professional skills to place children in a secure position to be able to collaborate in making decisions about things that affect their lives. These contrasting positions are constructed by very different sets of assumptions in two key areas. One is in the area of what it means to be a practitioner or a professional. The other is what we understand by childhood. Poststructuralism would refer to a range of discourses about childhood and professionalism. The contrast is presented in Table 3.1. The pervasive existence of discourses that are contrary to a rights position is what is most constraining of professional efforts to involve children more in decision-making.

There are, of course, other assumptions about professionalism and about being a child – the model in Table 3.1 is presented for simplicity in order to make a point about the effects of such contrasting positions. In reality the situation is far more complex. These

Table 3.1 Contrasting understandings (discourses) of childhood and professional role from different positions on participation

	Positions on participation	
Different discourses	*Rights*	*Protection*
Understanding of childhood	Child as active participant	Child as innocent and immature
Understanding of professional role	Professional as responsible for understanding complexity of situations to empower, facilitate and support	Professional as independent expert in a particular domain of knowledge and skills

discourses come to be understood as truths and help to construct the norms of professional practice. We are simultaneously subject to them and assist in their construction, and work in services whose systems also to varying degrees support them. Such complexity is explored in Chapter 6. This would also support Galloway *et al.*'s (1994) and Armstrong's (1995) suggestion that it may not be poor practice that led to a lack of consultation with children in the 1990s, but rather:

> the demands of a complex situation in which the needs of competing clients (school, parents, LEA and child) may determine the extent to which the child's perspective is allowed to be relevant.
>
> (Galloway *et al.*, 1994: 66)

Changing practice is not simply about developing the appropriate communication skills to talk to children. Galloway *et al.* (1994) found that even when a child remembered being asked for their views about their own education, they did not say anything: 'They asked me but I didn't say owt because I didn't know what to say.' Galloway *et al.* (1995, 1994) comment that not knowing what to say is not the same as not having anything to say. Shier's (2001) often quoted pathways to participation asks important question of professionals at each level: Are you ready to listen to children . . . To let children join in decision-making processes? Is there a procedure? Do you have a range of ideas? Do you work in a way that enables you to do these things? Are there certain ways that you work, certain frameworks of practice that are more supportive of the kinds of relationships you want to develop with children, and could you develop these practices further? And finally – is there an organisational obligation for the kind of involvement that is planned: is it a policy requirement? 'Just asking' children is clearly not enough. Chapter 6 takes this further arguing for the need for a higher level of political literacy on the part of professionals, to understand the different assumptions of professional practice, the different ways we think about people (about children and parents), and what we make of context. Speaking of context, it is worth being reminded, from socio-cultural understandings of childhood, that children and young people *are* active participants, whether or not we encourage this. They act in the world in ways that attempt to make active sense of what happens and to have some influence over events. The implications of this are that, whether or not we take actions to involve children in professional actions, they will actively construct what is happening according to the information available to them. We have seen, in this chapter, potentially damaging consequences that seem to arise when children and professionals act on incomplete information. There is no longer any choice about whether or not to provide children information and whether or not to involve children in decisions. The choice is on how to, how much to and what will be the outcomes for all concerned.

4 Parent partnership
The need for a richer story

I had to put an awful lot of effort in not to become powerless (mother).

She's not doing anything except what most intelligent, articulate mothers would do, which is to defend her child (SENCO about a mother).

It's not a matter of equality or expertise, it's a matter of mutual respect. You know, I don't think we should pretend we are all on a level, that kind of partnership. Or that we have equal parts to play. It's about becoming involved together, and honouring what each other can give. And they'll be different contributions (educational psychologist about working with parents).

(Todd, 2000a)

Introduction

There is no simple answer to the question of what kinds of interactions between parents and practitioners are likely to assist inclusion. A more involved relationship for parents with schools and services has been a growing feature of policy and practice over the last 40 years. But how far has this assisted the development of inclusion? An even greater role for parents in shaping schools is being planned, with LEAs being charged with becoming 'champions of pupils and parents' (DfES, 2005b: 11). There is a government aim to: 'transform our school system into one that responds better to the needs and aspirations of parents. Every parent should be confident that the system is delivering for their child. Every community should be confident that all parents can choose an excellent school' (DfES, 2005b: 11).

But how can this be achieved? What can help us to arrive at more clarity about the kinds of collaborations that should be sought with parents? This seems likely to require more open and creative conversations about what partnership is about, what we assume inclusive education to be, and the relationship between them. We know that the involvement of parents of children with certain kinds of special needs, especially if the parents have the backing of powerful voluntary agencies, can lead to more resources being secured for children in mainstream schools (Riddell *et al.*, 1994). However, this is only a small part of what inclusive education is about. This book adopts a definition of inclusive education that is wide-ranging and encompassing, that it is (quoting from Chapter 1) about the following: all children . . . valued equally, treated with respect and provided with real opportunities . . . responding to diversity . . . listening to unfamiliar voices . . . participation in . . . fulfilling potential . . . developing a fairer society. Rather than any single model of inclusive education, these definitions are likely to lead to lots of different ways of doing inclusion in schools. And rather than concentrating on one group of children, this book highlights any and all known exclusions, on the basis, for example, of disability, ethnicity, gender, sexuality, class and level of behavioural challenge to schools. This book's definition of inclusive education is one that assumes an active engagement of parents with children/young people and teachers and other practitioners. All key voices are required – in complex ways – to build inclusive solutions. What do we know at the moment about how we might define partnership with parents? Professor Sheila Wolfendale has consulted for years with practitioner and parent groups, and the following definition of partnership recurs in her writing:

- parents are active and central in decision-making generally and its implementation;
- parents are perceived as having equal strengths and equivalent expertise;
- parents are able to contribute to, as well as receive, services;
- parents share responsibility, thus they and professionals are mutually accountable.

(Wolfendale, 1985: 14)

Similarly, Gillian Pugh has consistently emphasised shared purpose, mutual respect and the willingness to negotiate (Pugh, 1989). Cross (1989) defines partnership as exchange of knowledge, common purpose and joint decision-making.

Despite considerable advances in professional involvement with parents, this chapter suggests that a partnership relationship has been derailed. This chapter's contribution is to review the current landscape of links between parents and schools and to discuss some significant ways that this has happened. A way of conceptualising these seemingly intractable issues is discussed in order to look at what might be needed to start to make real headway, so that partnership is more than lip-service.

Initiatives in parent partnership: is this inclusive education?

There have been numerous initiatives over the last 40 years that have involved practitioner links with parents around education. For example, there is a large number of important texts by Wolfendale, to take a key author in this area, on the links between schools and parents, most involving contributions from practitioners and other researchers. Some texts look generally to improve education for children (Wolfendale, 1983; Wolfendale, 1985; Wolfendale, 1992a; Wolfendale and Bastiani, 2000), others focus on literacy (Wolfendale and Topping, 1996), many are concerned to improve schools for children with special educational needs (Wolfendale, 1989; Wolfendale, 1992b; Wolfendale, 1995; Wolfendale and Cook, 1997; Wolfendale, 1997a; Wolfendale, 1997b; Wolfendale, 1997c) and there are also thoughts on parenting education and support (Wolfendale and Einzig, 1999). The emphasis of published work has moved from a more limited focus on special needs (Cunningham and Davis, 1985) to more recent texts that encompass the full range of excluded children (Beveridge, 2005). How far can we identify positive moves towards inclusive education in such initiatives? Parent initiatives can be roughly grouped as follows:

- *Family and parent learning* has been concerned with: family literacy programmes and parents delivering home-based reading programmes (Topping and Wolfendale, 1985; Topping, 1986; Topping, 1995); school sessions informing of their children's school curriculum more widely (Merttens and Vass, 1990; Merttens and Vass, 1993); and family learning days in which children and parents or other family members have a fun day on various activities (Cummings *et al.*, 2004: 42) or focused on one area such a digital photography or local history.
- *Family and parenting support* has usually referred to a broad range of programmes aiming to support parents in the endeavour of parenting (Wolfendale and Einzig, 1999; Moran *et al.*, 2004),

and can include parent-run support groups and structured pro-grammes aiming to train parents in particular techniques of parenting.

- *Parent involvement in assessment.* There is a growing call for parents to take part in their children's assessment more generally (Wolfendale, 1993), an aim for a role for parents in the Common Assessment Framework (HMSO, 2003: 71), and an obligation that has been in operation in different ways since the Warnock report (1978) (Mittler and McConachie, 1983) for parental contribution to statutory SEN assessment (DfES, 2001b; Wolfendale, 1995).

- *Parent participation in voluntary agencies.* There is a small but increasing number of parent-centred organisations (PCOs) or voluntary agencies, run by parents or involving a majority of parents, with a variety of aims. Some national organisations concerned with parents of children with special needs are very dependent on parent support, such as IPSEA (the Independent Panel for Special Education Advice) and Contact-a-Parent. Carol Vincent has written about a range of parent groups (Vincent, 2000; Vincent and Warren, 1997).

- *Parent partnership schemes.* Parent Partnership Services are now required in every LEA in England and Wales. These services are usually for parents of children who have special educational needs (SEN). The purpose varies, but tends to be concerned with: the reduction of conflict between parents and the LEA; an increase in the participation of parents in assessment through information, recruitment and training of named persons to support parents; and partnership with voluntary agencies (DfEE, 1993; Wolfendale and Cook, 1997).

- *Link worker, key worker or lead professional.* An overwhelming complaint of many parents of children with disabilities and with special needs is that they have to deal with too many professionals. This often means repeated assessments to access resources, too little information-sharing by professionals, and a lack of co-ordination of services (Dessent, 1996; Duncan, 2003; Greco and Sloper, 2004; Halliday and Asthana, 2004; McConachie, 1999; Sloper, 1999). This has been expressed as the need for joined-up services. One solution is the development of link workers or key workers to play a particular role in achieving such a service. The 'every child matters' agenda identifies a lead professional who takes overall responsibility for the case when a child is known to more than one specialist agency (HMSO, 2003: 53).

A case can be made that in all the initiatives listed above, some positive moves are being made towards inclusion. There is a preponderance of texts showing how increased involvement of parents in their own learning has had a positive impact on the engagement of their children in learning (Cummings *et al.*, 2004; Dyson and Robson, 1999; Macbeth, 1993; Merttens and Vass, 1993; Topping and Wolfendale, 1985) or how parent training programmes have led to changes in child behaviour or family functioning with a positive knock-on effect in schools (Moran *et al.*, 2004; Quinton, 2004). Parent partnership schemes can assist parents to be able to interact more effectively with the services involved in the statutory assessment of special educational needs (Wolfendale and Cook, 1997). There is no doubting the cumulative anecdotal evidence: studies quote many parents who feel more confident about their own learning, are able to play a greater role in their children's education, and are better equipped to be parents.

However, without detracting from the many achievements of these initiatives, one can ask of each: Is it partnership? and Is it inclusion? Long-term impact is often hard to demonstrate and the problems in schools of attendance, behaviour and underachievement continue. There are still major exclusions of children and young people. Making headway perhaps goes beyond ventures connecting parents and schools: it involves many changes internally within schools in how teaching and learning is managed. However, it is also possible to notice omissions from current associations parents have with education. What is often missing is reciprocity: where parents, children and young people play a central role and activities are not just led by professionals. Family learning and family support has generally been directed by practitioners with little part played by parents in shaping programmes. This is not supposed to be the case in some current developments. Sure Start programmes combine both family learning and support with the offering of other services to parents. An important aspect of such schemes is the involvement of parents in the planning and delivery of services. Extended schools similarly combine family learning, parent education and services for parents, although there has been little evidence of parents playing a role in service evolution (Cummings *et al.*, 2004). Vincent found that whilst PCOs made gestures towards 'counterdiscourses', and gave voice to sub-ordinate identities, interests and needs usually silenced (Vincent, 2000: 128) the fact that they were usually drawn from professional middle-class groups limited their ability to share 'capacity' and 'capability for agency' with currently disenfranchised groups (Vincent, 2000: 104).

Parent partnership schemes (PPSs) have been criticised for dis-empowering parents in their relationships with school. By forming the main link with parents, it is possible that PPSs remove schools from the arena of partnership when a child is being assessed for SEN, which may distance responsibility of schools to take seriously the need to engage with parents as partners (Todd, 2003a).

Why is it so important for parents to be fully in the driving seat alongside teachers and other professionals? It is argued here that unless threats to participation are recognised, any movement to develop rights and to put into place projects based on equal participation will only confirm existing inequalities, will not involve excluded parents and children and will do little to facilitate wider inclusive education. These threats are interconnected, but can be articulated as follows:

The first threat is a lack of *real* partnership. The *concept* rather than the *practice* of some kind of equal participation can be identified throughout policy on parent involvement in education. Current and past ways of working with parents have been based on some kind of normative notion of parents and of the ways parents link with schools. Anyone who falls outside these norms find it very difficult to find an active relationship with schools that fits with how they understand themselves – making hard to see how such parents can make a contribution to inclusion. Another assumption of much of the work that happens betweens parents and professionals is that parents are some-how lacking or to blame for difficulties. Once again it is difficult to see how partnership can happen or how parents can be agents in the development of inclusive education if they are regarded, through the assumptions of professional practice, to lack competence. This leads, therefore, to the other two threats to participation.

The second threat is a failure of practitioners to engage with parents as a diverse group and to devise a variety of ways to hear them and engage with them on their own terms.

The third threat is the a deficit notion of parenting that underlies most parent–professional initiatives and not recognising the need to find collaborative initiatives that do not pathologise them, but build on respect and trust.

These threats are explored in detail before looking at how they can be overcome.

Has partnership been happening?

In thinking about how to develop practice now, it is often very helpful, even briefly, to take an historical perspective. Where we have come from can be surprisingly influential for where we are going. The current notion of partnership has not always been a mantra of education and other services. The image of parents held by professionals and the defining guise of the relationship professionals and parents assume they will have with each other has changed over the last five decades. Prior to the 1970s, parents were primarily regarded as a 'problem' (DES, 1955: 77). In the area of disabilities, parents were either viewed as in need of psychiatric counselling to cope with grief from the birth of a child with severe learning difficulties (Read, 1985: 17; Sandow *et al.*, 1987: 12) or they were required to change, being seen as the main influence on their child's response to school (DES, 1967; Evans, 1975: 14). In the 1970s, parents started to be viewed in guises other than 'problematic': as teachers in a 'compensation' (Barton and Moody, 1981; Thomas, 1978), or 'transplant' model (Jeffree, 1980, quoted in Mittler and McConachie, 1983: 9; Topping, 1986). As clients, parents were allowed an honorary role of teacher in order to provide information and to carry out the advice of professionals, to enable professionals to use parents as change agents (Cameron, 1986; Daly *et al.*, 1985; Gliedman and Roth, 1981: 231; Newson, 1976; Clarke, 1982; Cunningham and Davis, 1985; Cunningham and Sloper, 1978; Mittler and McConachie, 1983; Mittler and Mittler, 1982). Such involvement also lies within a 'compensation' view of parents, casting them both as a part of the problem and as professional aides.

'Partnership' has been a growing theme in the overall relationship between parents and education, but also between parents and other services, over the last 50 years. However, partnership has meant several very different things, often at the same time. Bastiani (1987) classified parents' relationship to formal education into four different models: compensation; communication; accountability; and participation, as outlined in Table 4.1.

A number of key government-commissioned policy documents bear witness to the development of a discourse of partnership. However, when the detail is looked at, it has often seemed to depart from the equality explicit in Professor Wolfendale's definition of partnership. A close look at assumptions underlying the language used about parents suggests the reports discussed have all, to a large extent, assumed Bastiani's (1987) compensation or communication models of parental involvement in schools. Partnership was and is clearly on the agenda,

Table 4.1 Models of partnership

Model	Characteristics and assumptions
Compensation	An underlying belief that inequality in education might be overcome without structural changes, by changing attitudes. Parental interest crucial for achievement. Teachers have a task to facilitate greater involvement of parents, to make the least 'successful' families more like the most 'successful'. Deficit models of family life. Parents passive and an undifferentiated group. Parents need the involvement of professionals.
Communication	Parent involvement is dependant upon the level of information parents have about the school and about the progress of their child/children. Information understood to be largely un-problematic. The need to look for opportunities for communication and to develop them in their most effective form. Attention to practical arrangements for communication.
Accountability	Parents as consumers of education. Parents a major audience for education. Different models of accountability: parents an undifferentiated consumer group. Within this a discourse of choice over school, a concern for access to performance indicators (league tables published in national press).
Participation	Emphasises shared goals and complementary roles for teachers and parents, which assumes a partnership of equals. An ideal to aim for, representing a radical critique of home–school relations.

(From Bastiani, 1987)

but realising it in anything more than name has seemed to have been problematic. Partnership has primarily meant little more than co-opting parents onto the practitioner agenda, enabling the parent to play the role required by the professional.

This is demonstrated with reference to some of the key policy developments over the last 20 years:

- In the Plowden Report (DES, 1967), greater partnership seemed to be about improved information, communication and choice – only an element of how we would today understand partnership.
- The Bullock Report (1975), looking at teaching and learning in

literacy, endorsed the idea of parents coming into school to help with language activities (Bullock, 1975, para 5.37: 70). In many ways it too endorsed a compensation model, with a slight nod towards participation in the need to recognise parent perspectives.

- The Warnock Report (DES, 1978) continued the trend towards 'partnership' with parents. Not only did it, throughout, stress the need for 'the closest possible involvement with parents in the assessment of the child's educational needs and in the provision made' (7.18: 107) but an entire section (chapter 9) was devoted to parents as partners: 'It is a partnership, and ideally an equal one' (9.6: 151). However, the way that parents were framed in the body of the chapter on parents suggested, once again, Bastiani's (1987) compensation and communication models rather than participation. For example, many of the recommendations were concerned with facilitating information between home and school, but particularly from the school to home, and ways the parents could assist the school in its task. There was also a strong sense in which the parent was presented as *in need* (researcher's emphasis), in terms of coming to terms with the child's disability, or in terms of requiring practical help. There was no sense in which parents might have perspectives that the school or other professionals outside school ought to take on board.

Partnership with parents is – once again – an explicitly stated notion in the current delivery and development of schools and services. There is perhaps a welcome departure to some realism and clarity in more recent policy documents. The major policies of this decade are more specific in articulating what is being provided for parents and what role is expected. The discourse in the delivery of health services to children, and educational services in Scotland, is one of listening to parents and taking action: 'Children and young people and families receive high quality services which are co-ordinated around their individual and family needs and take account of their views' (DH and DfES, 2004: 87) and 'We will give parents and carers a better say in the education and support for their child' (Scottish Executive, 2003: 30).

In recent policy on schools and the development of services, parents are politically very much under the spotlight, with many nuances to the ways they are to be related to. The discourses are of catering for parents, providing support and ensuring their engagement, balanced with a discourse of choice over schools (DfES, 2004a; HMSO, 2003).

This contrasts with a very strong partnership discourse, meaning a more reciprocal relationship between parents and professionals, in the Code of Practice for SEN (DfES, 2001b) and the White Paper, with, in the latter, parents even being able to run schools (DfES, 2005b).

We think we do partnership – but it seems as if we do not. Why is this? What is getting in the way of partnership? Head teachers, teachers, and professionals involved in the delivery of services seem to carry out their endeavours with respect to children and parents very much on their own terms. They want the involvement and support of those who use their services, but within prescribed roles. This leads to a normative discourse in the relations between families and schools, a lack of attention about how to attract parents and how to work with them in a more reciprocal relationship. It is here that the chapter turns to next.

Is 'partnership' open to all?

'Parents' is a term so well used we rarely think about its meaning. One under-articulated aspect is the lack of homogeneity of parents – that all parents are different, and assumptions cannot be made about the perspectives or actions of 'parents'. This has important implications for practitioners. If the individual perspectives of different parents are not recognised, then home–school relationships may be diminished. Some parents are sent for, some are consulted, some fight for and get what they want, and others are forgotten. Practice, policy and research on home–school relations has largely been silent on the issues of gender, race, class and disability (David, 1993). The relative lack of involvement of fathers in their children's schools receives little attention (Garth and Aroni, 2003). Vincent argues that economic considerations are often ignored factors in home–school relationships (Vincent, 2000), as being involved in a child's school takes time, and challenging educational professionals requires cultural, social and ecomomic capital. Choice of school is limited by various aspects of cultural capital, particularly access to information on schools and physical proximity to particular schools (Gewirtz *et al.*, 1995; Reay, 1996) and so is not a 'choice'.

When it comes to class, it seems partnership eludes both working-class and middle-class parents (Crozier, 2000). In her study of parent and teacher perspectives on the relationships with schools, Crozier interviewed parents from 62 middle-class households and 53 working-class households. Generalising Crozier's findings, working-class parents seemed to want a separation between home and school, and generally trusted the teachers. However, they did not always find it possible to be involved with schools to the extent that they understood what was going on as this would mean 'being pushy', which would be stepping outside what constituted for them being a 'good parent'. Middle-class parents were more in evidence than working-class parents in making representations to the school to do with their children, and for the most part in finding a successful outcome for themselves. Crozier (2000) talks of middle-class parents more often having the 'upper hand' in relationships with teachers. Teachers did not seem to welcome this, and wanted middle-class parents to trust them, to 'let them get on with the job and leave it to the professionals (Crozier, 2000: 121). It is arguable that in neither case was partnership the model wanted or operated by teachers or parents.

Ethnicity is one of the most under-acknowledged factors disadvantaging parents in home–school relations. Crozier's ESRC research reveals little known understandings about the perspectives and knowledges of schools and home–school relations of parents who are of different ethnic groups living in areas in the north-east of England. Rather than hard-to-reach parents, Crozier (2000; 1996) argues instead for 'hard-to-reach' schools:

> the schools and in particular the secondary schools, are 'hard to reach' for many of the parents in our study because many expectations are assumed and thus 'hidden'. The emphasis within notions of 'involvement' does not include a sharing of views and ideas and in this sense lacks a sense of respect and albeit unwittingly gives out a message that the parents are not valued. Schools expend huge amounts of energy and time and resources sending out information to parents. The fact that it is not an effective way of 'involving' parents or empowering them to take a more proactive role has to be reconsidered. But we argue there is something more. The research evidence suggests that many of the schools are not sufficiently welcoming to these minority ethnic parents; not sufficiently so at least, to help the parents overcome their own apprehensions about their lack of educational knowledge, levels of English or even how they will be received as 'Asian' and Muslim people. The schools have also failed to address racist abuse towards their children (see Crozier and Davies 2007). Consequently, it is argued, the schools for many of the parents in our study, represent places which are insecure, are potentially hostile and are places where they are rendered vulnerable. In these ways therefore many of the schools in our study represent spaces

of exclusion; unwelcome spaces where few Bangladeshi and Pakistani parents have a voice.

(Crozier and Davies, 2007)

In related research, literacy practices, understanding of what reading is and what it is for, and how it is learnt, differed considerably for children culturally Bangladeshi in the LEA school and in the community classes outside LEA school time. In the latter, children participated in Bengali or Arabic classes to strengthen cultural identification and to learn religion (Gregory, 1994). It is hard to see how moves to involve Bangladeshi parents in literacy initiatives in school can succeed without an appreciation of parent perspectives on both literacy, parent links with schools and indeed on education as a whole. Similarly, Border and Merttens (1993) suggest that many schemes involving parents in aspects of the curriculum, such as paired reading, have the effect of camouflaging contradictions and conflict endemic in such situations as there is no evidence of attempts by schools to take on board notions of how families understand literacy.

Having a child with a disability or with special needs makes anything approaching partnership particularly problematic. Many parents of children with special educational needs are required, by the need to liaise with teachers over the assessment and education of their child, to have a relationship with schools that is different to that of other parents, and one they may not wish to have. Goodley *et al.* (2006) examined the care experiences of parents of babies and children needing specialist care and support in hospital and community settings. This research worked with 39 families, aiming to make their voices heard in debates around care provision, and co-ordinated six focus groups of professionals. They were particularly interested in looking at how parents and young children up to the age of 5 were treated by professionals in the care they received and how that helped or hindered their lives as families with disabled babies and young children. Their reports deserve full reading. For the purposes of this chapter they found parents were engaged in 'long-standing processes of negotiating, brokering and fighting for the rights of their children', and that 'parents generally struggle more with coming to terms with fragmented service provision than with the "disabilities" of their children'.

Parents of children with disabilities and special needs are also a diverse group and experience different inequalities. Sandow *et al.* (1987: 22) referred to 'customers' and 'suppliers'. Customers mark out those parents who have some rights in commenting on education, and are part of a consensus about the service on offer. Other parents simply supply their child and have little agency in their relationship with professionals. This refers to parents of children with special needs, but could refer equally to parents of children in other marginalised groups. Tomlinson (1981) distinguishes between parents that have been 'sent for and told' about their children's difficulties from those who have been 'consulted'. Chandler (1986) found differences in parent–professional relations between parents of children in different special needs placements. Interviews were carried out with parents of children in four different kinds of placement: schools for children 'with moderate learning difficulties', nurseries, residential schools for children 'with behavioural and emotional difficulties' and mainstream schools. The group who, when asked if they felt themselves to be partners in the assessment process, said they felt least involved as partners, were parents of children in residential schools for children 'with behavioural and emotional difficulties'. Parents of pre-school children gave the most favourable response. Similarly, Sandow *et al.* (1987: 25) found that parents of a child 'with severe learning difficulties' are likely to have a very different relationship to professionals from those with a child who has a reading difficulty first discussed when the child is 6 years old.

Children who have a disability and whose families also represent other disadvantaged groups are suggested to have even more difficulties in their relationship with a range of services, including education:

- Particularly high levels of unmet needs were found in families of children (categorised as) having very severe disabilities, those from ethnic minorities, families of older children and those who have more than one child who has a disability (Sloper, 1999).
- Even in special schools, the parents said, 'their children were not wanted because they didn't have the right sort of special need' (Duncan, 2003: 346).
- The lack of powerful pressure groups behind certain types of special educational need may lead to disadvantages in terms of securing scarce educational resources (Riddell *et al.*, 1994).
- Tomlinson (1982) suggests that professional attitudes towards parents in the area of special educational needs have been shaped by their social class status.
- A larger proportion of parents whose children are formally assessed for special educational needs on average have lower incomes and a mother not working (Sloper, 1999).

A lack of school choice for parents of children with special needs is enshrined in legislation due to the measure of discretion for each LEA to decide how to make the best use of resources by balancing the interest of both SEN and other children (Henshaw, 2003: 4).

> In all of our case study areas (i.e. in semi-rural as well as urban settings), parents of children with SEN perceived and found themselves to be marginalised and devalued by LEAs and schools as they attempted to engage with the process of school choice. Frequently, information and guidance were unavailable, limited in nature or untimely. School open evenings were often found to be unaccommodating and school managers and specialist SEN staff were sometimes unapproachable or absent.
>
> (Bagley *et al.*, 2001: 306)

Partnership, it seems, is conditional. It is not open to all. Even the version we have now, the 'transplant' model, one more about having some kind of connection with the school in order to support the teacher or another professional, seems not to apply to everyone. It is a one-sided contract, meaning that you sign up to the school's interpretation of what a home–school link involves. And if you have other ways in which you would feel more comfortable in interacting with the school, these only seem to be on the agenda with further problematising of parents as 'hard to reach'.

Deficit notions of 'parent' and 'family'

A major threat to partnership is the strong and enduring theme that parents lack competence:

> I hadn't worked since 1988 when my first child was born, so we're talking about quite a few years I had been a mum basically. I had lost an enormous amount of confidence over that time, not being in the workforce, not actually perhaps using my brain in that way to filter through the ideas and arguments.
>
> (Vincent, 2000: 132)

Further than this is the discourse that parents themselves are a problem, and are part of the child's problem. This can be traced in almost all home–school policy and research where families have children who are disabled, are from different ethnic groups, and are disadvantaged by low income. This theme highlights the deficit notion of parent skills, a lack of parent interest in their children and parent responsibility for the problems of their children (Todd and Higgins, 1998; Todd, 2000a). This runs counter to any kind of 'equality' assumed in a relationship of partnership.

The deficit view of parents of children who have special needs has a long history and has been referred to earlier in the chapter. This has cast parents as a problem, as not 'accepting' aspects of the child. There continues to be a strong professional perspective on parents as needing to be seen as grieving for and as having yet to come to terms with the child who is not, in some way, matching up to expectations (Read, 1985: 17; Sandow *et al.*, 1987: 12; Swain and Walker, 2003). Involvement with professionals has left parents seeing their austistic child in terms of deficits, as being very different from normal children in a way that left them feeling that their own perspectives were not listened to (Billington *et al.*, 2000). This view is strongly contested by many parents and has started to be contested in the literature (Dale, 1995; Sloper, 1999). Goodley and McLaughlin find that, as parents' understandings of their children are constantly developing and moving, it is unhelpful to view them as occupying fixed parental types e.g. 'parent in denial', 'parent in crisis', 'parent as difficult' (Goodley *et al.*, 2006: 4).

> Disabled children and their parents become the objects of scrutiny and separation from the moment impairment is identified, and identification leads to separation in terms of policy and practice. Irrespective of grand claims to inclusion.
>
> (Corker and Davis, 2002: 88)

Key inquiries into child abuse have been accompanied by a loss of innocence. The family was no longer to be regarded as an automatic place of safety for the child, not that this had, in reality, ever been the case for a large number of children. The family was no longer sacrosanct. However, there was some call, albeit far less voluble, for increased agency for the child. With increased state intervention in the family, the family has become a political football, open to blame and responsibility for almost any society ill or concern. With blame and responsibility came the assumption that the state can direct all kinds of intervention at the doorstep of the family in its effort to achieve political ends. Low achievement of children, seen largely as the failure of families to prepare children with the appropriate aspirations or verbal or literacy skills to be ready for school, has arguably led to a range of interventions from family literacy to extended schools. A project in Newcastle LEA which aimed to raise standards in schools in an area of disadvantage and underachievement was prefaced by a deficit model of parenting. An evaluation report (Easen *et al*., 1996) asked how it could ever hope to raise standards through one of its espoused actions, parent partnership, when the project was based upon a deficit assumption which ran counter to partnership. Anti-social behaviour of children and young people was and is firmly placed at the feet of parents with the state response being parent training classes to teach parents how to look after or to discipline their children. Such thinking underlies the current emphasis on parent support in the 'every child matters' agenda (HMSO, 2003). Parents are jailed for the non-school attendance of their children. Alongside the discourse of blame and intervention is the discourse of responsibility. This is a reminder to families, but of course primarily 'nuclear' families, of their importance in upholding 'values'. A fundamental value being the 'nuclear-ness' of the family. Parental involvement has been suggested to present a caricature of white, middle-class family life as an ideal and to fail to acknowledge the heterogeneity of parenting practices (Bailey, 1993). The closely connected discourses of deficit, blame and dysfunction can be suggested to be thin stories that hide the richness and diversity of the lived experience of people in whatever it is that we call a 'family'. That tacitly accepted 'truths' about families can be unmasked as myths becomes apparent with only a modicum of evidence from such lived experience.

There were early attempts to counter deficit notions. For example, Tizard and Hughes's (1984) research with pre-school children, comparing the interactions between children and parents with children and teachers, demonstrated 'higher levels' of cognitive challenge in home than in school, whatever the social class of the home. There have been attempts to counter the deficit notion in some education documents, such as the Elton Report (HMSO, 1989) and the Code of Practice (DFE, 1994). In the latter, schools are asked not to 'interpret failure to participate as indicating a lack of interest or willingness. Parents may feel they are being blamed for their child's difficulties when the school first raises questions with them' (DFE, 1994: 2.29: 13).

Certainly, Hughes *et al*. (1994) found 'many of the assumptions about parents which were suggested to underlie the reforms of the time did not match closely with the real views, experiences and behaviour of the parents most directly involved' (1994: 206). Hughes *et al*. (1993, 1994) followed 150 children through Key Stage 1 (5–7yrs) of the National Curriculum, ascertaining the views of parents and teachers in regular interviews over two years. They found evidence that parents' interest and concern for their children's education was not always recognised by the designers and providers of that education (see also: Crozier, 2000; Wolfendale, 1985: 4). Those who do not get involved directly in their child's education have often had well-founded reasons (Topping and Wolfendale, 1985: 4; Crozier, 2000). One of the most vivid pictures countering the deficit perspective of parents is contributed from the views of parents themselves, highlighting problems experienced by their children as arising from the context in which they live (Fox, 2004) rather than from characteristics of the family or child.

The impact of the negative discourse of parenting is that parents do not know how to relate to schools. Parents sometimes have to step out of the role of the 'good parent' in terms of the non-confrontational relationship schools expect to have with them in order to stand up for the needs of their children: 'you overcome it, and you do your utmost to work alongside and with the school . . . what I found was, I was doing that too much, and I had to step back from that and partner myself alongside David, realign myself with David' . . . I was too much partnering the school, if you like . . . Supporting the school. Which is what you think a good parent does. . . . (David's mother, Interview 3: 28).

Parents speak of the need to expend a great deal of energy and persistence to obtain the services they require for their children (Swain and Walker, 2003), and to enter into roles that others do not have to adopt, to become campaigners, managers of conflict, perhaps giving up work, feeling cut off from other parents (Brown, 1994: 237; Duncan, 2003).

It is hard to be a 'good parent', such are society's disciplinary regimes for what constitute parenting. Parents are imbued with blame and lack of competence. Good parenting is only conferred when it is performed, and supporting the school in its educational decisions about a child is one such performance. Partnership only seems possible when parents are supporting professional agendas, and in doing so the professional can award the parent with competence. Ergo, parents in conflict with the professional community risk being further demonised as 'bad' or 'troublesome', and a discourse of partnership seems particularly problematic. However, these discourses are resisted both by the rich lived experience of parents themselves and some of the research and practice that has made known the thin nature of some stories that exist in professional assumptions.

Conclusion

Current initiatives that aim to tackle inclusion through the involvement of parents are making some, though perhaps limited, progress with this aim. But there is little sign of anything like partnership in any widespread sense, if this means an equal and reciprocal relationship. Professional practice can be shown to be constructed by a range of understandings that have developed over time about what the professional role is about, and about many other areas, such as, in this discussion, how we think of the 'child' and the 'parent' or 'family'. It is as if a thin story of partnership has developed, that gains its power as it co-opts some other thin and dominant stories of professional practice and parenting. The dominant story of the professional as the source of competence and knowledge means it is very difficult to relate to those with whom we work without this being the driving factor in the relationship. Table 4.2 contrasts assumptions of professional role and parent for different conceptualisations of parent relations: partnership, transplant and compensation. So, even if professionals themselves reject the 'expert' mantle and try to involve parents in a partnership relationship, there are many discourses that run counter to partnership that are arguably more readily available.

David Galloway, Sally Tomlinson and Derrick Armstrong (Armstrong, 1995; Galloway *et al.*, 1994) suggested that parents involved in special educational needs assessments lacked the power to state their own views, and were likely therefore to be disempowered by professionals' attempts to bring them into partnership (Armstrong, 1995). In other words, partnership might simply make it more likely that parents go along with the professional's view of the situation. The same research (Galloway *et al.*, 1994) found parents often felt their contribution was only listened to when they were confirming professional views, and professionals seemed to direct them towards a consensus. The teaming of thin discourses, that parents lack competence, and that parents can acquire competence from professionals, means that parents are rewarded by a conferred identity of 'good' parent if they partner the professional.

However, in other ways we can see the performance of a range of alternative stories for the identities of professionals and parents. We can find a range of constructions of relationships between them that seems to be at odds with a narrow discourse of partnership where a professional agenda is what counts. A varied and multi-storied identity of parents as resourced and competent is readily available from any conversation with a parent. Stories of competence in the literature is found of all families (Weingarten, 1994), in families who struggle (Coll *et al.*, 1998; Seaman and Sweeting, 2004), and families of disabled children (Murray and Penman, 1996). Seaman and Sweeting (2004) criticises the perspective that non-traditional family forms are lacking in social and cultural capital, but shows how they actively utilise

Table 4.2 Contrasting assumptions of professional role and parent for different conceptualisations of parent relations: partnership, transplant and compensation

	Partnership	Transplant	Compensation
Description of relationship	Parents are active and central in decision-making, have equal strengths and equivalent expertise, are able to contribute to as well as receive services, share responsibility and are equally accountable.	Parents carry out tasks to assist the role of the professional – professional skills transplanted by those of the parent, with direction from the professional.	Parents regarded as a problem or in need. Professional expertise required to compensate for lack in parents.
Examples	Parent support schemes in which parents are fully involved. Family group conferences – parent resources recognised, family responsible for solving welfare and other problems.	Parents hear children read at home, help in the classroom, accompany school trips, attend parents evenings, carry out activities suggested by occupational therapists, speech and language therapists, educational psychologists etc. Family and parent learning programmes.	Many schemes for family and parenting support, particularly training programmes. Many family and parent learning programmes.
Role of professional	Professionals and parents together negotiate situation and what is required as a response.	Professionals identify the need and suggest solutions/ways forward/diagnosis.	Professionals identify the need and suggest solutions/ways forward/diagnosis.
Model of parent	Parents have resources, knowledge and strengths. Everyone has problems, and everyone has the skills and resources to solve those problems, sometimes in partnership with others.	Parents have limited resources, knowledge and strengths. This knowledge might be seen in defined areas, such as an in depth understanding of the child. Resources may be understood in terms of having greater time to work in more depth with the child.	Parents are a problem and are part of the child's problem.
Homogeneity vs. parents as having distinctive lived experiences	All parents understood to have distinctive lived experiences, different perspectives and understandings.	Parents treated as an homogenous group: the same invitations to support child's education issued to all. Parents treated as different, parents of children deemed to have particular needs (special needs, a disability) required to interact with school and professionals in ways different to that of many parents.	Parents in need targeted.

alternative support processes and network associations. Crozier researches two groups of parents often absent from research and pathologised in educational practice, working-class parents (Crozier, 2000) and those from different ethnic cultural groups (Crozier and Davies, 2007). She finds stories of interest and concern for their children's education and preferences (including hopes and fears) for their relationships with schools. Goodley *et al.* (2006) found parents of disabled young children occupy roles that are continually evolving and 'becoming'. They also found their understandings of their children to be constantly developing (as, indeed, it is with all parents).

The enduring life of the 'partnership' discourse, despite little success over the years, may offer a clue to the hopes of many professionals for a more respectful and reciprocal relationship. Chapter 6 offers the PPC Model that hopes to assist a move towards collaborative relationships between parents and professionals. Consistent with this model, ideas for ethical parent partnerships are proposed by Professor Sheila Wolfendale to enable practitioners to consider their relationships with parents:

> Some suggested areas/components for an ethical partnership between workers/practitioners/ teachers/professionals and families in service delivery:
>
> - statement of primary rights, responsibilities, commitment by the partners;
> - full knowledge and informed consent by the partners;
> - opportunities for family members to be involved in design and delivery of involvement/intervention;
> - individual and family rights not to be harmed, stressed, deceived, put at risk, exploited by their participation;
> - agreement over 'rules of engagement' (who does what, where, when, how, why);
> - a written agreement regarding involvement;
> - clarity and agreement over ownership of information.
>
> (Adapted from workshop discussion materials by Sheila Wolfendale, used in 2004 with EPs)

In order to achieve Professor Wolfendale's vision there is perhaps now a need for a more grown-up version of how relationships between parents are understood. Maybe current ways of thinking about 'partnership' have had their day.

5   Integrated services

An invitation to inclusion, or exclusion?

The simplicity of the idea is contrasted by the complexity of its implementation.

(Greco and Sloper, 2004: 14)

Introduction

What is the relationship between good multi-agency working and the provision of inclusive schooling? For inclusive education to be successful it seems obvious to state that professionals – teachers, other professionals in school, practitioners working outside schools, those working with voluntary agencies – must work together and in collaboration with children, young people and parents. There are lots of ways that professionals are currently working together in order to effect inclusive education in schools. Some of the most currently available models of practice, of childhood and of the parent/family mean that collaboration, between children/young people and professionals and between parents and professionals is not easy to achieve, as has been discussed in Chapters 2, 3 and 4. Moreover, effective multi-agency working does not necessarily lead to inclusive education – as it is focused on all kinds of aims and priorities, many of which have nothing to do with education, inclusive or otherwise. In the delivery of services to children, multi-agency working is being focused upon as never before. Agencies are being restructured to bring together the different services concerned with children, a process likely to take a number of years. Nationally funded initiatives, such as Sure Start, BEST teams, integrated community schools (Scotland) and extended schools (England), involve a range of professionals working together for a variety of different aims around a central social inclusion concern.

This chapter considers invitations for inclusive practice that seem to be emerging from the greater partnership working as a result of the development of integrated children's services. It suggests that without an explicit inclusion agenda that is reflected in how services are organised and practice is conceptualised, and without a high degree of political literacy, this massive increase in multi- and inter-agency working is likely to have, at best, an accidental impact on inclusion, and at worst to substantially lose ground already gained. Multi-agency working will only assist inclusion if it facilitates: the rich storying of the identities of children and young people – but also of professionals – through an inclusion of the voices of children and parents; a challenge to the deficit and blame perspectives of children, families and communities; and a response to social injustices. This chapter considers why this is the case and some key issues for restructured services if they are to continue to assist the development of an inclusion agenda.

This scrutiny of professional culture is *not* to place blame on professionals. It is to suggest that there are a range of social practices that shape our interactions and that we join with them in complex ways. These may not be the intentions of or reflect the beliefs and values of those who work with children and young people, but it is in the ether, the fabric of our institutions, in the spaces between us. Awareness and reflection can lead to it being more easy to join with those discourses that *do* reflect professional beliefs about participation and inclusion.

'Integrated services' may mean more multi-agency working – but is it inclusion?

In Scotland and England the major reorganisations of services and agencies for children both have strong social inclusion agendas (HMSO, 2003; Scottish Executive, 2001; Scottish Executive, 2003). The definition of inclusive education, assumed by this book as discussed in Chapter 1, is sympathetic with social inclusion. However, as will become clear later, 'social inclusion' as a term has a role to play but is too broad and vague, and the author's definition goes further, as it is actively critical of excluding practices and:

> is about responding to diversity; it is about listening to unfamiliar voices, being open, empowering all members and about celebrating 'difference' in dignified ways. From this perspective, the goal is not to leave anyone out of school.
>
> (Allen, 1999: 14)

However, if services and agencies *were* able to play a role in tackling social inclusion, this would represent a significant step towards the kind of culture needed to bring about inclusive education.

Within a strategy of integrated children's services, extended schools (England) and integrated schools (Scotland) are seen as ideally placed for the delivery of reconfigured community services in order to achieve social inclusion (see Chapter 7 for a case study on extended schools). There are mutually dependent rationales for schools and other services to be part of this re-organisation:

- The core purpose of the school, that is, pupil learning and achievement, where the communities of schools face significant social and economic disadvantage, cannot be achieved 'simply by standard measures to improve the internal management and practices of the school' (Dyson *et al.*, 2002: 7). At the very least, such schools have to work particularly hard both at the 'internal' issues, such as teaching, and at their 'external' relationships with their parents, communities and community services.

  > An extended school maximises the curricular learning of its pupils by promoting their overall development and by ensuring that the family and community contexts within which they live are as supportive of learning as possible
  >
  > (Cummings *et al.*, 2004: 4)

- Area regeneration cannot happen without schools playing a central role as part of a co-ordinated strategy. There are various differences in emphases in a rationalisation for such a role: the school having a part to play in community problems and family support; the school as significantly responsible for developing social and cultural capital in communities; and the school having an impact on employment and local economic development (Dyson *et al.*, 2002: 8).

As suggested by Cummings *et al.* (2004), we can think of extended schools as operating across a territory which is more extensive than that within which schools have usually defined their role. The ways they work across that territory will depend upon partnerships in other agencies and services, and will vary from school to school. Table 5.1 defines the territory of extended schools in terms of three levels at which the schools can operate – individual, family and community – and three domains in which they operate – educational, social and health. The core business of all schools is where individual and educational interests intersect, that is in enabling pupils to learn within the

Table 5.1 The territory of extended schools

Domain	Learning	Social	Health
Pupil	Curricular learning Extended opportunities for learning Individual barriers to learning – behaviour and learning difficulties, truancy, underachievement	Personal development, aspirations, engagement, social well-being, attendance, criminality, abuse, public care	Well-being, healthy living, sexual health, substance misuse, physical illness, mental illness, disability
Family	Family support for learning	Family functioning, parenting skills, family support, child protection issues, housing issues	Family functioning, parenting skills, family support, family health practices
Community	Community opportunities for learning Cultural attitudes to learning Social problems impacting on learning	Crime rates, community safety, community capacity building, housing, leisure, transport issues, employment opportunities	Community stress and well-being, community safety, cultural health practices, environmental health

Key
Core concerns of schools
Factors bearing directly on student learning
Factors which facilitate and support student learning
Factors with indirect impact on student learning
(Cummings *et al.*, 2004: 20)

curriculum. However, the ways pupils learn will be influenced by such aspects as the pupil's personal and social development, their aspirations, family support for learning, and the pupil's health. These bear directly on a pupil's learning – and extended schools takes such factors into their orbit. Beyond these are factors that may be agued to have a less direct influence on learning but are none-the-less influential. They are also factors over which schools have a less direct influence. This includes family health, housing, and employment. It is likely that any action in these 'less direct' areas will call for collaboration with other agencies and organisations. Cummings *et al.* (2004: 21) suggest that a map such as that in Table 5.1 can assist in planning – who is already doing what, how much of a territory needs to be covered, how individual activities offered by an extended school build up into a coherent strategy, and what else an LA partnership will plan to do.

This sounds easy and, perhaps, makes sense. There seems an implicit assumption that social inclusion will be the logical conclusion of the achievement of major agency reorganisations with extended schools at the centre. But this is by no means necessarily the case.

Too much to achieve and inclusion a low priority?

The integration of children's services requires changes that are numerous, headline and time consuming. They can all arguably fit within a social inclusion agenda, but may be incompatible with the educational focus and the assumption of participation explicit in the author's definition of 'inclusive education'. Furthermore, there may simply be too much to achieve for inclusive education to have a chance in being heard.

The listed aims of the 'every child matters' agenda (HMSO, 2003) have become guiding principles for health, social and educational services for children, including schools. The overall aim is fully compatible with 'inclusive education'. There is a requirement to ensure that every child 'has the chance to fulfil their potential by reducing levels of educational failure, ill health, substance abuse and neglect, crime and anti-social behaviour among children and young people' (HMSO, 2003: 11). The government has set out what it considers to be a positive version of the outcomes they want to achieve, which are: being healthy, staying safe, enjoying and achieving, making a positive contribution and economic well-being. The agenda also urges that 'raising standards in schools and inclusion must go hand in hand' (DfES, 2004c: 36). However, in the re-organisation of children's services, the actions that follow from the need to develop services that are protective and preventative are not necessarily consistent with the development of inclusive education, or raised standards in education.

There is a strong argument that current moves to integrate services have their origin in the recurrent investigations into child protection tragedies since the 1960s. Inadequate progress in inter-agency collaboration despite recommendations from successive enquiries (DHSS, 1982; Hallett, 1995; HMSO, 1988) solidified resolve for change after the tragic abuse and death of Victoria Climbié in 2000. Whilst the aim to prevent child tragedies has now been combined with the wider aim of reducing social exclusion in society, it is proposed that child protection will always take precedence. The aim of protecting children from harm can certainly be understood to be inclusion in terms of including children in a culture of care and enabling children to take part in society free from abuse. Not wanting to detract from this, if preventing child tragedies is the key underlying aim of multi-agency working, this is not likely in itself to have any effect on inclusive education.

Integration of services requires a great deal of attention from professionals to set up and use new systems, develop ways of working and evolve management structures. Part and parcel of the drive towards improving services for children and avoiding child tragedies of the past is the creation of information systems that enable services to track children and the services they are accessing. This has involved a parallel priority, the negotiation of a common assessment framework for all services. The aim to organise more effective services has led to other tasks, other priorities, in the provision of 'seamless' services for children and parents. A relatively new role has been created to co-ordinate services, that of the lead professional. This role also assists in keeping track of the child and co-ordinating the use of the common assessment framework at the level of the individual. A seamless service provided by well-coordinated agencies using a common assessment framework will not necessarily also deliver inclusive education. It is difficult to see, given the complexity of changes, how professionals will have time to also focus on inclusion. Structurally and radically re-organising whole agencies and services represents a masterly attempt to try to tackle some immensely complex problems. There is, however, a danger that it is trying to achieve too much at once, and that other important aims, such as inclusive education, will get lost.

Systemic medical model

Almost any attempt to summarise the intentions of the 'every child matters' agenda is likely to oversimplify, given the far-reaching nature of its reforms of policy and structure. However, it is fair to say that the key vehicle for achieving the five positive outcomes, with the two overarching tenets of prevention and protection, is through the effective offering of services. This could be termed a 'service delivery' emphasis. All the other changes lead, eventually to this. Effective delivery seems to be understood in terms of services being offered early enough (early intervention, rapid response delivery), via partnership between services (with a lead professional and partnership working to ensure no duplication of services or passing between them), in places easily accessible to children, young people and families (i.e. in full service extended/integrated schools), delivered by people with the correct skills (workforce reform), and with a graded response so that services are both universal and targeted. There is a well-articulated aim to organise services 'around the child, young person, or family, rather than the existing professional functions' (DfES, 2004c). Many local authorities are tending to test their newly visioned structures by imagining a child or family with a problem and tracing through the kinds of services that would be available to him/her/them. Once again, the focus is on service delivery. Integrated services in Scotland, whilst different in several areas, share a similar emphasis.

However, there is a serious flaw. Such a model implies that the child or the family need fixing. In essence, this is a *deficit* rather than *strengths* approach to people and their situations. It is, in effect, a systemic embodiment of the medical model. It is as if the system conspires to see all problems as inherent to the individual rather than as a complex interaction of social practices and institutional, political and cultural influences. It is difficult to see how such a model can support inclusive education. Something fairly fundamental is being said here. It is not just that the inclusion aim competes with other aims, such as child protection, but that the core, the way services for children are conceptualised, is flawed in terms of the possibilities for inclusive education.

The different professionals involved in the system need not hold with a medical model for the system to operate as one. This may not even be an intended effect of integrated services. Indeed, it was stated at the start of the chapter that social inclusion is an overall motivation for making such far-reaching reorganisations. These are major systemic interventions that aim to align with social inclusion and emphasise the need to intervene in a joined-up fashion in communities in order to solve entrenched problems. But, in making so many changes at once at a time of reform, it is not unexpected that the new system would start to exert its own character that might not be in keeping with other intentions. An example of how the 'systemic medical model' works in practice is presented before looking at further implications of this model and ways of dealing with it.

Joint Action Teams: an activity system

The ways that a service delivery model might unwittingly operate as a systemic embodiment of the medical model and support excluding practices can be understood by analysing some multi-agency teams using an 'activity system'. The analysis was carried out by a group of 15 educational psychologists working in a council in Scotland who were part of a number of different multi-agency groups. 'Joint Action Teams' is one of the names given to the new multi-agency teams developed in integrated community schools in Scotland. They are similar to those already existing in many schools, and newly formed in others, as ways to bring the perspectives of different agencies to bear on the needs of particular young people. In this case these teams included teachers, relevant non-teaching practitioners in school, social workers, education welfare officers and educational psychologists. In other schools, a wider range of professionals might be involved. Typically, the different professionals would consider the cases of individual young people, sometimes with and sometime without the presence of the young person at the meeting. Different professionals would state their knowledge and involvement with the young person, give details of any assessments and interventions, and a discussion would lead to some kind of action plan for the young person. It would be likely that future professional roles would be specified, in terms of direct roles in working with, meeting with, the young person, and who would have an indirect role, perhaps finding out about further resources available.

To look at the relationship between a service delivery model and inclusion, the working of the JAT was explored using activity systems (see also brief explanation in Chapter 1 of activity systems). Activity systems (based on socio-cultural historical psychology) do not look at actions or thoughts as the main unit of human functioning, but are instead concerned with 'activity', referring to the whole system that connects the person concerned with a problem area, the object or goal via some way of achieving that goal, some kind of mediated action changes (Daniels, 2001; Engestrom, 1996; Engestrom, 1999; Engestrom *et al.*, 1999). The activity cannot be understood apart from its socio-cultural historical context, so aspects that reflect this context are considered. This includes the community (individuals who share the same object), rules (tacit and explicit norms that influence the activity), and division of labour (the way tasks and power is divided between those involved with the activity). By mapping out all these elements of a problem or of a situation, people can be assisted to find ways forward. The activity system is a tool that can be used by practitioners to reflect on their work and make changes in the direction of desired outcomes, and it is also used as a research tool. There are several examples of its use in understanding education (Leadbetter, 2004; Boag-Munroe, 2004; Daniels, 2004). It is a tool that, in the carrying out of the analysis through discussion, enables practitioners to understand more about the whole picture of a complex set of circumstances. In discussion to decide what aspects of a situation are to be placed in the particular parts of the triangle, practitioners seem to experience realisations about the processes at work in a multifaceted situation involving different people and different contexts.

Figure 5.1 shows the kinds of elements that are placed at the vertices and mid-points of sides of a triangle. The situation is 'separated' into object, outcome, subject, tools, rules, community and division of labour (Daniels, 1998: 104). They are mapped according to the following definitions:

Object – raw material, problem space at which activity is directed and which is moulded and transformed into *outcomes* with the help of tools;

Subject – the individual or sub-group whose agency is chosen as the point of view in the analysis;

Tools – artefact, instrument, means relating subject to object to produce outcome, physical, symbolic, internal, external, signs;

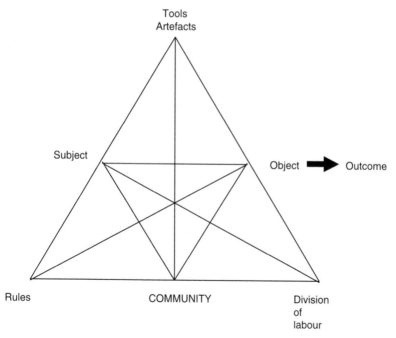

Figure 5.1 An activity system.

Rules – tacit and explicit regulations, norms, and conventions that constrain actions and interventions within the activity system;

Community – multiple individuals and/or sub-groups who share the same general object, who may not be where the subject is, who constructs self as distinct from other communities;

Division of labour – horizontal division of tasks between members of the community, and vertical division of power and status.

In the current discussion, the activity system allows multi-agency working to be located within the physical and institutional context, according to the social roles and status of the individuals involved, and in the context of the cultural mediators available. It allows a focus on certain areas of the complexity, in a way that relates to other aspects of human activity found in other contexts. It allows more theoretical analysis of what is actually happening when professionals work together.

The educational psychologists who devised this activity system (see Figure 5.2) were interested by what they found. The process of mapping out the elements of the system enabled a discussion of the hidden assumptions of the meetings and the potentially excluding processes in an element of practice that was assumed would contribute to inclusion. The child 'Kirsty' is the subject, and the objective is the achievement of an inclusive solution via a multi-agency meeting. Tools, the medium of relating the subject to the object, is interaction, talk. The main discoveries were the 'rules', the norms, tacit and explicit assumptions that were present at the meeting. Rules depicted represent only a selection – far more were possible given more time for discussion. The main realisations about what the hidden 'rules' were calling the professionals to join with were as follows:

- a bias towards finding a solution that further labelled the child;
- finding a way for the child to be the responsibility of professionals other than school staff;
- to have a placement, even temporarily, that removed the young person from the school's concern;
- a focus only on problems;
- the young person seen solely in deficit terms;
- no real place in the meeting for the voice of the child whether or not the young person was actually present or not at the meeting.

This analysis therefore demonstrated to the educational psychologists possible ways in which the social practices that support such teams

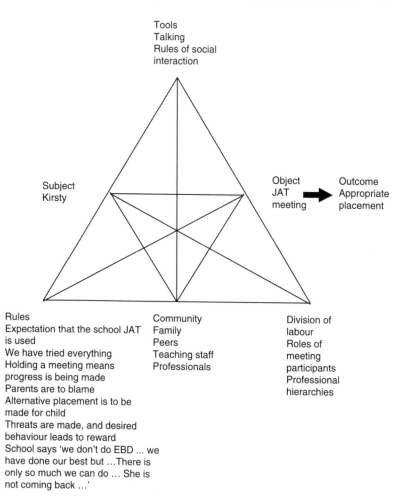

Tools
Talking
Rules of social
interaction

Subject
Kirsty

Object
JAT
meeting

Outcome
Appropriate
placement

Rules
Expectation that the school JAT
is used
We have tried everything
Holding a meeting means
progress is being made
Parents are to blame
Alternative placement is to be
made for child
Threats are made, and desired
behaviour leads to reward
School says 'we don't do EBD ... we
have done our best but ...There is
only so much we can do ... She is
not coming back ...'

Community
Family
Peers
Teaching staff
Professionals

Division of
labour
Roles of
meeting
participants
Professional
hierarchies

Figure 5.2 An activity system of a Joint Action Team meeting.

might unwittingly draw professionals to excluding practices. The activity system appeared to enable the psychologists to be more explicitly aware of things they knew already and so be in a position to reflect on how to approach JAT meetings in a way that sat more comfortably with their values and interests. Systemic impediments to inclusion, and the discourses that limit possibilities for children, seemed to become more visible through this process: '[in education] the only model of support consistently applied is the response to acute problems and often involves some form of exclusion' (Milbourne, 2005: 679).

What kind of multi-agency working is good for inclusion?

Doing multi-agency working *better* will not necessarily improve inclusive education – especially if assumptions inherent in the system are inconsistent with inclusive education. We need to explore what is meant by 'better' – and *better* for what *purpose?* Applying the principles from available texts on how to do good multi-agency working to services delivered to children will, hopefully, assist professionals to work together around a shared aim, or to negotiate when there are a number of conflicting agendas. There has been a great deal of attention given to ways to improve multi-agency working. We now know quite a lot about how to do this. Indeed the current reforms in children's services aim to tackle much, in terms of structural impediments, that has long been said to stand in the way of inter-agency collaboration. There is also more understanding about what impedes professionals from working together – and what needs to happen to facilitate joint work (Roaf, 2002; Townsley *et al.*, 2004; Atkinson *et al.*, 2001; Capper *et al.*, 1993; Kendrick, 1995; Lloyd *et al.*, 2001; Roaf and Lloyd, 1995; Stead *et al.*, 2004; Wigfall and Moss, 2001; Dyson *et al.*, 1998; Easen *et al.*, 2000). Caroline Roaf (2002) identifies characteristics of good inter-agency practice as involving the following:

- formal commitment and support from senior management and from political to practitioner level;
- formal and regular inter-agency meetings to discuss ethical issues, changes in legislation and practice, gaps in provision and information-sharing at all levels to develop short- and long-term strategies;
- common work practices in relation to legislation, referral/ assessment, joint vocabulary, agreed definitions, procedures and outcomes;
- common agreement of client group and collective ownership of the problems, leading to early intervention;
- mechanisms for exchange of confidential information;
- a framework for collecting data and statistical information across all agencies that can inform all practice, including 'ethnic' monitoring;
- monitoring and evaluation of services in relation to inter-agency work;
- joint training in order to understand each other's professional role.

(Roaf, 2002: 87)

The list of characteristics of good inter-agency working are helpful and important. However, knowing them draws our attention to what is still not known, or to questions that remain unanswered. We have little clarity about how practitioners need to work together to bring about any particular aim. What is long overdue is a more clearly focused consideration of what is distinctive about the ways that agencies and professionals need to work together to bring about inclusive education, rather than other professional aims and agendas. This is explored in the next section looking at two examples from multi-agency practice.

The context vs. individualisation: two examples of practice

In the remaining sections of this chapter, the aim is to open up for exploration, and at the same time deconstruct, an understanding of what 'individual' and 'context' might look like. There is a history of finding it tricky to resolve the relationship between the individual and the context, whether context is understood (in a reductionist sense) as 'the environment' or in terms of one of many different ways of conceptualising culture. This has been the case from early nature vs. nurture debates to the current understandings about the medical model vs. social inclusion, which seems to pit a concern for the individual against an awareness of contextual influences. The intention in the remaining sections of this chapter is to start to move away from such dichotomies altogether. The suggestion is that for multi-agency working to effectively contribute to inclusive education, there needs to be a culture of practice in which these are not seen as separate, but in which the individual is understood in terms of some kind of thinking about 'context'. First we return to current thinking on integrated services within a social inclusion agenda before considering two examples of practice.

One way of thinking about integrated services is that different agencies should have as their main concern different aspects of the life of the child, family and community. The school is, by this way of thinking, concerned with learning; health professionals deal with health issues; and social services professionals focus on family problems. Each agency deals with one aspect of the individual, whilst others can be left to sort out one version of context. For schools, the social and health needs of the pupil, the learning needs of the family, and the health of the community in which the pupil lives could be seen as 'context', to be addressed by agencies other than that of the school. This is one interpretation of Table 5.1. However, the suggestion here is that this would be an inadequate way of dealing with and conceptualising situations, and in particular an over-simplistic way of looking at the 'individual' and at 'context'. According to such a way of thinking, people would be objectified and separated into parts that do not seem to fit with the interconnected ways in which life is lived. An alternative way of thinking is suggested. Table 5.1 might be thought of as a way of viewing the complexity of issues that impact on learning, but not as a way of allocating responsibility to different agencies. We could still accept that the pupil as a learner remains the core concern of schools, but we could also suggest this might not easily be seen as a focus on the 'individual'. We could suggest that pupil learning cannot be understood without thinking about and action within, for example, family learning and health. In other words: perhaps we cannot think of the individual without the context.

If we are to avoid binary oppositions, we may need to start by paying attention to both the context and to the individual in a way that avoids the pitfalls of each, and without ignoring the other. What might this look like? This means paying attention to the individual – to the pupil in the classroom and to the child or parent in the consulting room – without taking up the invitations of blame and beliefs about the problem being located in the child and family that seem readily available in a medical model. This is likely also to signify being concerned with contextual issues when looking at problems that are often framed in individualised ways. On the other side of the traditional dichotomy, it means not losing sight of the individual when considering the context. This implies working with a conundrum – a central assumption that problems cannot be understood as individual in origin or in solution and yet a realisation that there is an individual that one is working with.

An exploration of two examples of inter-agency working suggests some of the important qualities of the ways practitioners might work with each other and with parents and children that might pay attention to both context and to the individual – to further inclusion. One is a study of an inter-agency initiative – 'Including Primary School Children' (IPSC), which ran from April 1999 to April 2002 in one inner-city LEA in England (Milbourne, 2005). The second is a study looking at inter-agency work to prevent school exclusion in three local authorities in Scotland. This was a Joseph Rowntree Foundation study conducted from February 2000 to April 2001 (Stead *et al.*, 2004; Lloyd *et al.*, 2001). In neither example were extended schools referred to, but both examples are consistent with the kinds of working now developing in extended schools. The purpose of referring here to families from Milbourne *et al.*'s research and the multi-agency meetings in the research by Stead *et al.* is to illustrate points being made here about how we might develop multi-agency practice for the aim of furthering inclusive education.

The primary school project was funded by the local Health Action Zone (HAZ) and consisted of three staff: a clinical psychologist and an educational psychologist (both full-time) and a voluntary sector social worker (half-time). They worked in eight primary schools managed by the three managers of the different staff. Each worker was allocated to one or two schools where they worked for one to four terms. The researchers interviewed the three workers, line managers, parents and children. Different kinds of meetings were observed: individual and group intervention work, class sessions, family conferences and case meetings. The perspectives of five mothers is reported in the research literature (Milbourne, 2005).

The study looking at inter-agency work to prevent school exclusion, in three Scottish local authorities, was a Joseph Rowntree Foundation project conducted from February 2000 to April 2001. Stead *et al.* (2004) and Lloyd *et al.* (2001), carried out 150 interviews in 6 schools, observed many meetings, and analysed the files of 30 case-study pupils. They compared multi-agency meetings in these different areas and found marked differences in the tacit rules and assumptions of the meetings. The researchers made comparisons between different ways of structuring multi-agency meetings in schools in two LAs, referred to as Douglashire and Walace city (Stead *et al.*, 2004).

Paying attention to the individual

A range of factors that show signs of being consistent with the development of inclusive education were identified by the author in the HAZ project, and many of these seemed to be about some kind of importance being given to the individual. Parents were reported to value a flexible and informal response. The researchers found that one parent valued a response that was 'tailor-made', 'so personal' (Milbourne, 2005: 686) to their situation. To the child of another the worker seemed to offer a refuge in the school. One parent's comments, reported by the researcher, suggested the worker was able to help her to communicate with the school when the parent felt she did not know what was happening for her child in the class. It was reportedly important to another that the worker was able to observe her children in both the home and school situation. Detailed consideration of her child in the class was suggested to be too time-consuming for the teacher, and she valued someone appreciating how the child was at home on a daily basis. These aspects of help seemed only available to the parents as a result of this initiative – they were not universally available.

In the study of LA inter-agency meetings, there were some interesting differences in how 'individuality' might be understood. Douglashire meetings had a case specific remit and were attended only by those involved directly with pupils. Meetings were characterised by careful adherence to guidelines, the involvement of the young person and parents, and limited available resources for young people. The advantages of this way of running meetings was suggested to be that there was a feeling amongst all participants of problems shared, that young people said they valued hearing things face to face, and parents felt problems were being taken seriously. These meetings respected the right of the young person and parents to be directly involved in decisions, and gave due regard for confidentiality. However, hidden rules included:

- schools have not tried everything and are passing on responsibility for the young person;
- professionals need to be careful what they say at the meetings; and
- no time for professionals to tackle their own differences face to face.

As a contrast, Walace city meetings were attended by key agencies, people who had worked together for a long time, such as school, social work, educational psychology, community police, and local voluntary agencies. Professionals who were directly involved with young people whose situations were being discussed were also present. The young person and parents rarely attended the meetings. Hidden rules of these meetings included:

- open and honest sharing of information including the anecdotal and speculative;
- a supportive and empathetic meeting atmosphere;
- discussions couched in good nature and humour, shared responsibility, not letting go;
- moving on to imaginative strategies when normal procedures were exhausted or seen as inappropriate; and
- a wider strategic role in developing policy and practice more generally.

There were a large number of resources available to the Walace city team to offer the young people. Most team members did not carry case loads or have statutory responsibilities but had flexibility to act on organise solutions and to intervene directly in cases. Open and frank discussions and innovative decisions were supported by the shared trust and shared histories of professionals, by abundant available resources and by the wider remit of the meeting (i.e. not solely focused on cases). However, confidentiality was an issue and young people and parents had little active involvement.

Meetings in Douglashire were concluded to be 'highly individually based, focusing on details of the lives of pupils and families . . . [and the] . . . contribution of professionals was more limited and less likely to produce informal, innovative suggestions' (Stead *et al.* 2004: 51).

However, there was, it seems, a recognition inherent in the practices in evidence in Walace city meetings that success was not a process of matching the resources to problems. There was a discourse of the rich storying of the young person, that:

> there were certain things that worked for particular young people but there were no simple answers. Some of the things that worked were to do with the skills and the characteristics of the workers, sometimes they were because they were there at the right time in a young person's life and sometimes they worked because everyone just kept trying, 'still hanging in there' (assistant head teacher, Braehead). Plans or strategies worked when they were the right thing for the young person at that time – when they were individualised responses.
>
> (Lloyd *et al.*, 2001: 71)

We may need to draw a distinction between taking account of the rich diversity of people's individuality (Walace meetings) and highly bounded, case-based discussions that individualise people's problems (Douglashire). It may be the latter that is associated with a medical model, and that it is the former that is helpful to the development of broad solutions that take account of context. Parents in the HAZ project reportedly valued the individual approach of the workers that took account of their personal situations. Similarly, taking account of the individuality of children/young people and their situations was important for the success, the creativity, of the Wallace city meetings.

In both projects that aimed to prevent exclusion, the HAZ project in primary schools and the study of LA multi-agency meetings, inclusive practice identified in both seemed to involve a flexible, creative response to people's lives that took greater recognition of the rich lived diversity of what it means to experience being children and families. In Walace and Douglashire it seems likely that other aspects of how meetings were structured made possible the differences between them in how the 'individual' was conceptualised and worked with.

Paying attention to context

In the study of multi-agency meetings in different LAs (Stead *et al.*, 2004) those in Wallace city seemed more able than those in Douglashire to understand problems as a function of the wider context, and to combine a consideration of individual situations with the development of policy and practice. One important implication of this is that it is indeed possible to structure meetings so that context is more of a focus whilst not losing sight of creative solutions for the individual: 'The case based approach (of Douuglashire) meant that problems were more likely to be individualised, seen as inherent in pupils, rather than in the practices of school' (Stead *et al.*, 2004: 49).

The value of intervening in the context appeared to be an assumed aspect of the HAZ project and to be recognised by both parents and workers. It seems appropriate to draw the conclusion, from the report in the literature (Milbourne, 2005), that parents using the HAZ project valued the assistance of the workers in intervening in the context, the environment, of their children's education – for example, through the improvement of communication with the schools, through the provision of a refuge for one of the children, and via listening to the parents, and other things referred to but not listed in the article (Milbourne, 2005). Some of the things both parents and workers thought were needed by the child's situation, signalled the requirement of a broad focus. For example, there was reference to a child being bored at school and more than one parent complained about the lack of continuity of teachers for their child. Another referred to the problems of the estate. One parent wanted help to be embedded in the school itself, rather than something special provided. Similarly, one worker noted that exclusion was often the result of support not being easily and universally available on site. One of the parents noted themselves being drawn in to focus on the child's behaviour, the school treating behaviour and learning as discrete difficulties. Each of these areas suggests (respectively) a different 'aspect' of context, not separate aspects – interrelated in complex ways:

- the quality of teaching and learning in the school;
- the living environment of the family;

- the kinds of resources available at the school; and
- the implicit 'rules' for dealing with problems.

In terms of the project on LA multi-agency meetings, the level of resources reportedly differed between Walace city and Douglashire, as did the 'rules' for how meetings were organised.

It seems we may be able to intervene with the individual in a creative way and at the same time to have regard for a range of contextual concerns. Contextual issues are clearly on the agenda for workers and parents. However, whether this is adequate to tackle inclusion is unlikely, particularly given the difficulties, looked at next, in making headway with the contextual agenda.

Falling into the trap of the dichotomy

We have seen in the previous sections clear examples of appropriate attention paid both to the individual and to the context in the HAZ exclusion project in primary schools and in the research looking at inter-agency meetings research on exclusion in LAs. However, invitations to the medical model are never far away. Support was still aimed primarily at the individual child and family. The individualised strategies in the HAZ project had little impact on institutional problems such as being a school in a disadvantaged area, facing problems in the level of school resources or in getting help from support services. By focusing interventions on the need for the child, parent or teacher to change some aspect of the child's behaviour, or the parent or teacher's management of the child's behaviour, there was an emphasis on 'individual inclusion' (Milbourne, 2005). When the particular help needed by one of the mothers, a parent support group, could not be found within the statutory agencies this led to further problematising of the mother by the system: 'Since many strategies focused on what the individual child and family could do, it was easy, as seemed to happen to Janet, once IPSC ended, for the parent or child to take on the blame for the failure if the strategies did not continue to work' (Milbourne, 2005: 686).

Similarly, focusing support at the level of the individual and family intervention:

> individualises the path to re-entry into mainstream activities and reinforces individual blame for failing to do so, presenting school difficulties and exclusion as deficits in a child's or parents' abilities than the deeper rooted problems of social inequalities.
>
> (Milbourne, 2005: 691)

A model that concentrates on making sure a service is reliably delivered to a person is unlikely to draw attention to systemic solutions. A 'service-delivery' approach may offer an anger management course when what is required instead is something that gives attention to social practices, or to organisational, political, social or cultural influences. This might be the challenging of institutional racism or the provision of an appropriate curriculum. But such challenging of context is not easy. The efficient delivery of targeted services is likely to be more consistent with an individualised client focus and to mitigate against the needed wider collaboration to tackle social structures. Easen *et al.* (2000) found inter-agency collaboration more easy to achieve where there was an individualised focus:

> the deep-seated economic and social problems of the estates on which they worked required successful collaboration in more open-ended community-focused, and longer-term contexts – that is precisely those in which effective inter-professional collaboration was proving so difficult to achieve.
>
> (Easen *et al.*, 2000: 365)

Participation – the defining issue

Participation is suggested to sit on the individual-context hyphen. It is the often hidden, usually ignored, element that resolves the dichotomy. If when we pay attention to the rich diversity of people's individuality and if we are fully involving the person in service evolution or decision-making, then we are unlikely to fall into the trap of blame and deficit. A response to the individual is not complete without recognition of the parent's or young person's agency in defining themselves, defining the problem or identifying the solution. Losing sight of the individual, whilst paying attention to the context is not possible if children/young people and parents are involved in defining and naming the context. Perhaps one of the clues as to why, despite paying attention to the individual and to the context, both projects were not as successful as they might have been in avoiding the traps of each, is that participation was lacking in different ways.

In terms of participation in the HAZ project, from what was reported by Milbourne (2005), the impression was given that the voices of the mothers and children were particularly available to the workers. One reason for this seemed to have been that his initiative provided time that appeared not to be available to teachers or other workers.

In Maggie's case it was important that the help she received was not something which the school or another agency had imposed on her. She had been involved in discussing the problems and possible solutions.

(Milbourne, 2005: 686)

However, the HAZ project did not, it seems, involve parents in the evolution of its ways of working in schools. In Douglashire young people and parents were heard at meetings and valued hearing things face to face but they rarely attended Wallace city meetings. However, imaginative strategies that appeared to meet the individual responses of young people seemed more available to Wallace city meetings than those in Douglashire. This raises questions about the way the knowledge of children and young people about their lives is given agency in professional situations.

the two models of school based inter-agency meetings present a paradox where the rights to participation of children and their families may be in conflict with the ability to offer flexible, innovative and informal practice. The dilemma for policy makers and professionals is how to resolve this so that informal creative practice can also promote accountability, confidentiality and the right to participation.

(Stead *et al.*, 2004: 51)

However, it is clear that the inclusion of voice in meetings is problematic, and the direct attendance at particular meetings by children and young people may not be the only way to achieve it. This is not only an issue in meetings, at the micro level, but is also a problem in how families and communities are defined at the level of the project – the initiative – or the school or service. The characterisation of the communities in disadvantaged areas in essentially negative terms, and the fact that such characterisation is by professionals, with little recourse to the perspectives of the communities themselves, is noted in the literature on extended schools (Cummings *et al.*, 2006; Cummings *et al.*, 2004).

Concluding thoughts

There are now exciting opportunities for schools and services to be in a position to grasp the challenges of social exclusion – to start to put in place solutions that take into account social, political and economic complexities. As part of this, systemic reorganisations of services for children are boldly taking on the structural barriers, in terms of the ways services are separately organised and funded, that have long been seen as a challenge to effective multi-agency working.

There is a lot of talk in multi-agency development of breaking down barriers and removing silo mentalities. However, we still know very little about what to do with something we may call a multi-agency team. In what sense is it a team? What is the import of the different disciplines or professional backgrounds? For some managers it is the breaking down of professional identities that constitutes an effective team. For others, those from different disciplines are thought to offer distinctive skills to clients with varying needs. A recent review of multi-agency working in Scotland suggests we have very little evidence to inform such ideas (Brown and White, 2006). Exceptions to this include research by Edwards looking at the learning that takes place across organisations (Edwards, 2005). Milbourne (2005) suggested greater advantage could have been taken of the project's multi-agency context, as the practitioners seemed to work very separately in each school. The capabilities of the whole team, or of the large range of people in services outside the team, were not within easy reach of children, families and staff at the school. However, what would this have meant if they had obtainable? What are the different skills and knowledge that parents and teachers might have found useful? However, it does seem likely that some of the qualities each of the three HAZ project members were able to offer the families were as a result of the multi-agency qualities of the team: such as the flexibility in action, autonomy in response, and being able to liaise without time delays with the teacher and with other services.

Service delivery needs to be more efficient – people need a quick referral when help is required – and there should be a better co-ordination of services. The demand for this is agreed by professionals, parents and other service users. However, the culture of service delivery is one that individualises people's problems. Therefore more efficient service delivery – including all the ideas of Roaf (2002), Edwards (2004, 2005), Dyson *et al.* (1998), Brown and White (2006) and Tisdall *et al.* (2005) and others – without efforts to avoid individualisation risks embodying a medical model even more than before. Examples from two projects that aimed to tackle exclusion were drawn upon to demonstrate that professionals/practitioners/workers do indeed work in ways that recognise the agency and diversity of the individual. Both parents and workers act together in the space of the context, recognising that problems are constructed by the context.

Whilst professionals and parents may understand the importance of context and the dangers of individualisation, it seems very difficult to avoid unwittingly joining with medical discourses of blame or the internalisation of problems. Finally, and centrally, participation is almost an after-thought, but is found in this analysis to be the pivotal link that avoids individualisation.

Chapter 6 presents a model of participative practice for professionals to use when working together that has at its core a critical approach to practice. Greater political literacy is needed about what it means to structure multi-agency actions – meetings and other events – so that what happens in schools and services moves further in the direction of inclusive education. Collaborative practice with children/ young people and parents seems to sit uneasily within many of the current ways we structure agencies working together – and yet we present participation as fundamental to inclusion. In Chapter 7 the theoretical ideas from Chapter 6 are taken into some examples from practice.

6 Participation for inclusion
The Practice–People–Context Model

Introduction

Inclusive education is about all children and young people. It is about their families, teachers and the other professionals whose work impacts on education. It is about how all these people 'respond . . . to diversity . . . listening to unfamiliar voices' (Allen, 1999: 14) so as to bring about 'the participation of learners in and reducing their exclusion from the curricula, cultures, and communities of neighbourhood mainstream centres of learning' (Booth, 2003: 253). Inclusive education cannot happen without participation. Participation, real partnership, involves children, young people and parents taking an active and central role in the development of schools and services, and an active and central role in decision-making in schools. It involves professionals working together to place children and parents in a position so that they understand the role of the person they are seeing and are able to take a full part in decision-making in services. Throughout, it is suggested that problems cannot be understood as individual in nature or in manner of solution, and that individualisation needs to be challenged. What follows from all these considerations is that schools and services can evolve in ways that responds to the perspectives and needs of the people who belong to these communities – resulting in inclusive education supported by inclusive services. In essence this is community psychology – the development of ways of working collaboratively, between practitioners and community members (Kagan *et al.*, 2006). The challenge for this chapter is to explain with respect to theory how this can happen so that the 'agent of change is communal' (Morgan, 2000: 31) and all knowledges are given voice.

This chapter is in part the conclusion – as 'conclusion' is not in the nature of things – of a gradually progressing story that has evolved throughout the chapters of this book. Here, the author brings together ideas and interprets them, speaks about them, through the PPC Model – the Practice–People–Context Model. This is a 'theory–practice' framework to aide a critical unravelling of how we work. It aims to communicate clearly what seem to be the fundamental ideas, assumptions and practices that appear to support collaboration. As such it is in itself a kind of theory, and underlying the framework is a range of diverse theoretical ideas that are also communicated within this chapter.

The good and bad news about participation

There is certainly evidence of collaborative practice in schools and services. Children and young people's voices have become progressively more audible in public life (Chapter 2). Excellent practice has been in evidence, with no shortage of ideas about how to enable child participation in schools and services. A growing literature charts the evaluation of participative experiences by children themselves. Children have been consulted about government policy, are involved at every level of operation in some voluntary organisations, have varying opportunities to make changes in school life via school councils and their perspectives are increasingly the subject of research. We have had parental involvement in schools for many years, a massive range of initiatives and examples of some good practice (Chapter 4). There has been an increasing focus in all agencies on multi-agency working (Chapter 5). The integration of children services in education, social care but also health offers a unique opportunity to further user participation.

However, collaboration is not widespread and is problematic. The child's voice remains, in general, absent from schools and services. Children have little involvement in the ways schools and services are delivered and developed. Some voices are heard less than others, particularly the very young and those with disabilities (Chapter 2). When it comes to children's use of services in health, education and welfare, there is very little evidence that children are put in a position that they understand the roles of people they see in such a way that they can play an active part in consultations (Chapter 3). Children and young people have views on what they want in schools and services they experience. They also have ideas about how they want to be involved and consulted. The close analysis in Chapter 4 of what is actually happening between parents and professionals reveals that partnership has essentially been there in rhetoric rather than reality in most home–school initiatives. Much has been achieved – but it is not partnership. And much remains to be achieved that collaborative working could go a long way to facilitate. Parents have been regarded as helpers to the professional agenda. Insufficient attention has been given to the individual stories of different parents such that many parents have been excluded from relationships with practitioners. Much of practitioner engagement with parents where there are concerns about children have been predicated by deficit assumptions about parents. The increase in multi-agency working will not necessarily contribute to improved collaborative practice with parents and children or to inclusive education (Chapter 5). Indeed there are grounds for thinking that inclusion is far down on the priority list of particular groups of professionals and of integrated services. Furthermore, there is evidence that the systems being developed by integrated services operate in ways that make both collaboration and inclusion less likely – as they appear, in most instances, to be operating a systemic medical model.

There is a keen desire not to move the 'blame' discourses that are usually applied to parents and children/young people and to 'dump' them, instead, on professionals. It is not the case in any simple sense that one set of people is oppressing another. It is that social practices are available to us all in complex ways – and that whatever the personal intentions of practitioners, it is not always easy to join with the practices that are likely to fit well with our intentions. Sometime we join unwittingly with excluding assumptions. We may reject individualised ways of working with people, but if the agencies we are employed by operate a systemic medical model then various assumptions will come with the person even before we engage with them. 'Professionals are often frustrated by barriers that exclude them working within a wider context of service provision' (Goodley *et al.*, 2006: 5). What this book – and particularly this chapter – aims to do is to explain more about why this is the case at the same time as offering a map – the PPC Model – to help punctuate what happens now with critical practice. The ideas developed in successive chapters and summarised in the PPC Model aim to provide a form of evidence that helps professionals to experience the interruptions needed to find more collaborative relationships:

> The development of inclusive practices involves collaborative working arrangements; that they can be encouraged by engagement with various forms of evidence that interrupt ways of thinking; and that the space that is created through such interruptions can enable those involved to recognise overlooked or, indeed, new possibilities for moving forward.
>
> (Ainscow *et al.*, 2003: 227)

The PPC Model: Practice–People–Context

Different strands of influence on our attempts to participate

In trying to understand why participation is so elusive, what is happening when it is working well, and what might be the central ideas to concentrate on in order to 'do more participation' in schools and services, three pivotal areas have emerged from the thinking and from the research drawn upon. These are three sets of considerations: about people; about practice; and about context. The discourses that help create our understandings and actions around each of these – the sets of practices that cluster by these headings – seem fundamental to what it means to be a professional and have quite decisive implications for participation. This has led therefore to the development of the PPC Model (Figures 6.1 and 6.2, and also Tables 6.1–6.3) which may help explain the threats to and possibilities for partnership. As in Easen *et al.* (2000: 366), this model is an 'attempt to impose order on this complexity without simplifying it out of existence, so that professionals can understand more fully the tensions within their attempts at collaboration'.

In the PPC Model, we can understand participation in terms of three dimensions – or sets of interacting practices – that shape schools and services at the macro level, and professional practice at the micro level. These are:

- Conceptualisations of *Practice*: discourses of practice, how we understand roles, the different frameworks and agendas that inform our practice.
- Assumptions about *People*: how we understand people, what assumptions we have about children, parents, families and workers.
- Relationship with *Context*: the meaning given to the context, how we understand the relationship between the individual, meaning either ourselves or those with whom we work, and the socio-cultural context.

Figures 6.1 and 6.2, and also Tables 6.1–6.3 depict different aspect of the model, and the following text explains its working, and implications, in more detail.

We can think of 'Practice, People and Context' as different dimensions. We can also think of them as sets of social practices. The aim of Figure 6.1 is to show them as sets of practices and different groups of

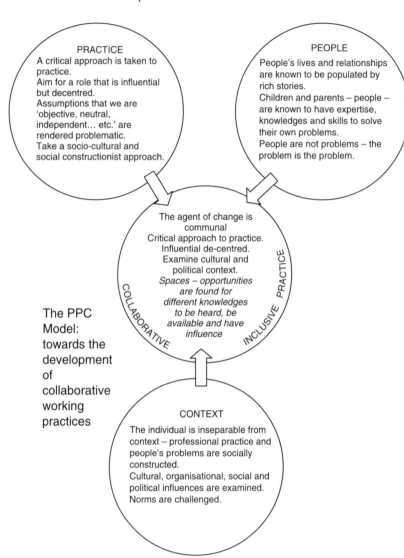

PRACTICE
A critical approach is taken to practice.
Aim for a role that is influential but decentred.
Assumptions that we are 'objective, neutral, independent… etc.' are rendered problematic.
Take a socio-cultural and social constructionist approach.

PEOPLE
People's lives and relationships are known to be populated by rich stories.
Children and parents – people – are known to have expertise, knowledges and skills to solve their own problems.
People are not problems – the problem is the problem.

The agent of change is communal
Critical approach to practice.
Influential de-centred.
Examine cultural and political context.
Spaces – opportunities are found for different knowledges to be heard, be available and have influence

COLLABORATIVE

INCLUSIVE PRACTICE

The PPC Model: towards the development of collaborative working practices

CONTEXT
The individual is inseparable from context – professional practice and people's problems are socially constructed.
Cultural, organisational, social and political influences are examined.
Norms are challenged.

Figure 6.1 The PPC Model: towards the development of collaborative working practices.

assumptions that are likely to be readily available when the aim is to develop collaborative working. The outer circles might suggest the assumptions of ways of working that might encourage participation, and the inner circle might speak to what the group overall is aiming to achieve. It is assumed in Figure 6.1 that the central concern, for any situation, project or organisation that has designs on the development of inclusive education, that seeks therefore to have a participative ethos, is that spaces are found for different knowledges – of children/ young people, parents, and workers – to be heard, to be available and to have influence.

The figure is applicable to a range of situations at different levels. It could depict considerations for restructuring services and could facilitate debate about how to avoid falling into the trap of becoming a systemic medical model. Or, the central circle might refer to the purposes of a project to provide better services to children with disabilities and their families or to young people in public care – and the assumptions about people, practice and context (the outer circles) could refer to the ideas that might inform such a project if it was trying to highlight values of inclusion. Or Figure 6.1 could simply refer to a multi-agency meeting, or to an interaction between a group of children, a teacher and a mentor.

Tables 6.1–6.3 explain about each dimension, suggesting what they might consist of – and the implications for partnership of the varying compositions. The separate depiction of Practice, People and Context is not to assume the detachment of any one from the other, but to enable some assumptions and ideas about each to be articulated. In reality, these filters are not free-standing, they merge into and are part of each other. As discussed in Chapter 5, the individual cannot be understood separate to the context. Furthermore, the lack of any clear boundaries should become apparent as they are described.

We can also conceptualise these three – Practice, People and Context – as different filters through which we see (see Figure 6.2). In the same way that if we were to wear glasses filtered red, we would see every colour very differently, we can think of the ways we look at our work

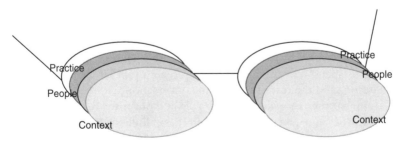

Figure 6.2 PPC Model of participation in professional practice.

in terms of different filters. What we place in each of the three dimension can act as filters for how we construct our professional life – how we look at issues, people and problems. The filters can have a cumulative effect – and one can contradict or support the other, leading to the vagaries and complexities in professional perspective and action. The filters might vary for us in different situations.

Practice: conceptualisations of practice

Some discourses of professional practice seem more likely to support a collaborative relationship with children and parents than others. In Chapters 3, 4 and 5 an understanding of practice as, respectively, independent expertise, as responsible for identifying need and solutions, and individualising the child and family were discussed in relationship to threats to participation and inclusion. If the lens through which we look when we construct our work is one that is solidly formed with an assumption of, for example, our own neutrality and independence, this may make it very difficult for us to look at our own practice as 'political', as constructive of identities, sometimes problem identities. Some of the headline assumptions of practice and their implications for partnership are summarised in Table 6.1, and some of these are further expanded upon in the following text.

The unhelpfulness of neutrality, objectivity, independence and action

One of the most unspoken discourses of practice that is unhelpful to professionals who work to develop participation is neutrality, accompanied by objectivity and independence. The assumed neutrality of those who work with children and young people is unhelpful for a discernment of what happens between professionals and their clients. Fundamental assumptions of professional working are rarely explored in order to gasp how to achieve any particular aim. There is a value placed on action rather than on reflection, research, debate and theoretical thinking. Imagine the reaction if, on Monday, instead of hitting the ground running to deal with the latest exclusion, a worker sat down to spend half the day reading research looking at ideas about exclusion, and the rest of the day in conversation with team members about what they thought was their role and purpose? Associated with this lack of value given to critical reflection, discussion and research is an assumption that professionalism is not to be questioned and interrogated. However, other forms of knowledge, including parenting and

Table 6.1 The implications for partnership of alternative assumptions about Practice

Assumptions of Practice

Against partnership	For partnership
Assuming a monopoly of professional expertise. Strategies designed by practitioners to sort problems.	Assumptions that one's role is influential. A 'de-centred role'. People hold the expertise over their own lives and relationships. The agent of change is communal, find what knowledges, of children, parents and practitioners, are present and enable these knowledges to have influence.
Assumptions of professional neutrality, objectivity, independence and action.	Awareness of political role of the professional, personal and professional agendas, range of clients. A valuing of reflection, critique, discussion, research and subjectivity.
Operating within a medical model – problems are seen as part of identity.	A socio-cultural and social constructionist perspective is taken.
Transmission view of education. Teaching staff set the agenda in schools.	Transformation view of education. Pupils have a role to play in setting the agenda in schools.
Teaching – learning relatively non-influential. Understood as a process of conveying the curriculum.	Teaching – learning process assumed to be influential and to be a process of personal change for pupils and teachers.
A non-critical approach to professional practice.	A critical approach to professional practice.

what it is like being a young person, are open for all to critique, so much so that they are rarely acknowledged as forms of knowledge. This is a problem for the development of participation in client–professional relationships and in schools in any initiative or policy, small-scale or large – even, as we see here, in the policy to develop extended schools:

> Those professionals are currently steering the development of community oriented schools on the basis of assumptions which are largely unquestioned and the implications of which are rarely

if ever articulated. Moreover, this cannot be seen simply as a failure of professional integrity. Given the multiplicity of forms of community-orientated schooling across the world, the tendency of the international literature towards breathless advocacy and, above all, the lack of serious engagement with fundamental issues in government guidance, professionals have little more to rely on in circumstances where they are required to respond rapidly to national initiatives, than their own best judgements.

(Cummings *et al.*, 2006)

Professional expertise as a cultural deterrent to partnership

The demands of effective communication can conflict with received notions of how professional/patient interactions should operate, and professional roles will need to change as relationships between providers and service users are redefined on a more equal basis.

(Clare and Cox, 2003)

The status of the professional has come under pressure in the last decade from inspection processes and bad practice publicised by the media. However, professionalism is still assumed to have the traits of: independence of judgement and practice; the offering of a disinterested service; a claim to a distinctive body of knowledge, skills and expertise; operation as an individual practitioner networked to colleagues; a monopoly over practice with control over access to expertise; and an ethical code of conduct and standards of practice policed by an organised body (Johnson, 1972). Further discussion of the history of different professional identities and theorising on the role of the professional can be found in other texts (Hugman, 1991; Johnson, 1972; Larson, 1977; Perkins, 1989; Perkin, 1996; Webster and Hoyle, 2000).

What are the implications of these traits for the development of collaborative working? For partnership to be possible, there is an implicit assumption that there is a recognition of equivalent but different areas of expertise. However, in a society where the parental role is devalued in comparison with the role of the paid worker and an implicitly assumed lack of competence is pitted against expertise and knowledge, equal partnership on this basis is unlikely to occur. The fallacy of the 'equal but different' argument is exemplified by the following quote from the author's research from the parent of David, a 7-year-old who was being formally assessed for a statement. There were differences of opinion between the head teacher, the parents and the other professionals involved about the nature of his difficulties. The parent comments on trying to have her perspective heard:

> on your own as a parent . . . it's very hard to argue it, it's very hard to say no my child isn't naughty he has a problem . . . it's a very dangerous sticky wicket and you feel very isolated . . . it's only when other professionals are involved that can look at it objectively perhaps. . . . I could say he had a fine motor problem and it was causing his behaviour problems, or some of them until I was blue in the face but until the doctor had tested him and said yes it is an actual thing, I was powerless really. . . . It's the actual help with Mrs B first thing in the morning that I think's made the difference. I think the other things [the actual formal assessment] have helped to change attitudes . . . (David's mother).
>
> (Todd, 2000a)

> I had to put an awful lot of effort in not to become powerless (David's mother).
>
> (Todd, 2000a)

David's mother felt unable to cross, unaided, into certain aspects of the professional role. Whilst she could label David as having a problem, she needed the other professionals to support her view and to define the learning problem in more detail. In order to strengthen her position she chose to co-opt with the viewpoint of professionals who were part of the assessment but outside the school and to adopt their reports for herself. Alone, she was not able to have a view that was respected and listened to. This is not to cast blame on the actions of individual professionals – it is a comment on the strongly held societal beliefs about professionals' expertise that make little room for partnership. In this situation as it happened, the child's educational psychologist was a strong believer in parent partnership and in listening to parents, but even this could not enable the parent to feel listened to within the social practice of assessment.

David's mother was able to find a way, via selective use of different professionals, to have her views of David's problems heard. Research looking at the processes that occur in meetings, suggests her experience might not be unique. It found unspoken rules about the order people were allowed to speak and what they were expected to talk about (Marks *et al.*, 1995). Professionals were expected to speak first and make expert pronouncements about the child whereas the mother was expected to speak last and make descriptive statements about the child that supported the perspectives of the professional. The vast difference that there sometimes exists between perspectives of parents and teachers is aptly described in Roffey's analysis of the views of teachers and parents about their respective roles and the ways they see the child (2004).

The competing nature of claims to authority from the professional against those from the family or the child, can be exemplified by considering the case, publicised in the media, in May 2004, of a 14-year-old girl who had an abortion following consultation with health workers, without the knowledge of her mother. The press portrayed this as the law coming between the child and parent, with headlines such as 'The State can never replace a loving mother' (*Daily Mail*, 14 May 2004: 13). There was much debate about whether the state can intervene in family business, or whether the family is the sacrosanct domain of the parents. There was a very real media 'battle' between the different 'rights': of the mother to know about her daughter and to give support; of the young person to have confidential medical information, to take her own decision on her pregnancy and on whether to tell her parents, and to have anonymity from the press; and of the professionals to follow legal procedure in giving confidential information. In this case the legitimate exercise of the professional role was firmly decided in terms of giving confidential information to the young person. That this became such a well-publicised case demonstrated that the understanding of the family as the unit holding responsibility, and therefore power, over the welfare of the child was fiercely debated. That, whilst professional practice did not in this case support such 'family rights', other elements in our current society disputed this – and indeed fought to give support to the power of the parents over the power of the professionals. It is argued that in this particular situation the professional, rather than the young person or the parent, carried the most authority.

Pervasive power of the medical model as an inhibitor of partnership

We expect professional actions to create solutions to people's problems. Our belief in professional independence obscures the ways the discourses of professional practice let us see only certain aspects of a situation in certain ways, and enable only certain kinds of communication to be possible. The medical model is suggested to be a significant discourse in professional practice, whatever individual approaches and frameworks adopted by any particular professional or worker (see

Chapter 5 for the systemic medical model). The broad medical discourse supporting all professional practice is that a person is assumed to have a problem, a problem personal to themselves, and experts are required to find a solution. The views of parents and children are rendered invisible by such a discourse. Gameson *et al.* (2005) have shown the implications of the medical discourse by looking at the discourse that surrounds some current terms and labels used by a range of professionals. Labels and terms include: conduct disorder, oppositional defiant disorder, attention deficit hyperactivity disorder, hyperkinetic disorder, psychiatric problems, psychological problems, mental health problems, personality disorder and emotional and behavioural difficulties (Gameson *et al.*, 2005: 51).

The discourses associated with these terms, essentially discourses of the medical model, are those that make child and parent participation in solutions very difficult to achieve:

- These tend to imply within-person problems and solutions.
- They pathologise, 'psychologise' or 'psychiatise' children.
- They tend to focus people's attention on symptoms and the need for treatment or cure.
- They are likely to disempower teachers, parents, children and other service users.
- They are based on the idea of linear cause and effect.
- They tend to imply the need for a specialist or an expert.
- They make change less likely or possible.

(Gameson *et al.*, 2005: 51)

This is not to deny there is medical, psychological, physio-therepeutic, social work, occupational therapeutic and many other forms of knowledge that may assist in solving problems. However, the power of these knowledges is such that other forms of knowledge – principally those of children and parents and other adults in the community – are often devalued or fail to be heard. The challenge, that will be returned to later in this chapter, is to find a way for all knowledges to be available.

Professional practices as creators of identities and 'image fixers'

The discourses of professional practice have the potential to create identities in unintended ways. Evidence of the ways children's identity possibilities are influenced by professional systems is provided by Stephen, who, on hearing that the placement favoured by the professionals for him to attend a residential unit had been rejected in favour of the preference of his parents for him to go to a different school said: 'now I'm not going to be naughty because I'm not going to the unit. They said I don't have to go to the unit any more. Then I can start being good' (Galloway *et al.*, 1994: 61).

Many of the systems professionals work within seem stuck to a discourse of 'difficulty' and 'problem', focusing on the negatives of a child, family or situation. Or it may be the case that the 'decision to initiate the assessment, because it reflects a particular view of the child's needs which then becomes the starting point for subsequent negotiations, may itself lead to the disempowerment of the child' (Armstrong, 1995).

Children – and families – present a varied, complex, and contradictory picture to the world. Partlett (1991) suggests professionals working with children are confronted with complex, ambiguous incomplete data and their professional frameworks invite them to reduce ambiguity. A consequence of this, it is suggested, is that selective aspects of a child are noticed and worked with:

> In freezing the image, observational data – already multiply transformed – are set down and become part of the child's history and record. These then become the currency of interchange between professionals . . . As a picture is built up, it gathers a momentum of accumulated opinion that becomes difficult to countermand, especially where there is little tradition of professionals' challenging one another's judgement.
>
> (Partlett, 1991)

Indeed there is evidence that the arena for professional action seems to be characterised by agreement and convergence of opinion rather than by challenge and debate at both an institutional level and at a case level, resulting is less critique of professional systems and institutions (Cook *et al.*, 2001: 142–143; Hallett, 1995; White and Wehlage, 1995).

Galloway *et al.* (1994: 151) found that it was more likely that decisions about the educational placements of pupils with behaviour problems would be 'negotiated between professionals, as well as between professionals and their "clients" in pursuit of a range of professional, political and pragmatic objectives'. The main role, therefore of the multidisciplinary assessment was to 'provide an arena for these negotiations' rather than to centre attention on the voices, agency and resources of the child or young person.

If society devises categories of children and attaches meaning to those labels, there is a high likelihood that we will find children to attach to those categories. Those children will have complex identities, skills, resources and problems, like the rest of us. But certain things will be noticed about the child in professional contexts such as schools. McDermott speaks about the *acquisition of a child by a learning difficulty* (1996). Discourses of professional practices can assist what Michael White refers to as a 'reproduction of the known and familiar': a reproduction of normative assumptions people make about themselves and that others make about them (workshop notes). 'Assessment plays a social function in the construction of identities of the child and interventions by professionals contribute to the construction of these identities' (Armstrong, 1995).

Cultural ideas about the purpose of school and what learning and teaching are about

We have come a long way from the time in the medieval period when monks were often the only educated members of society. But what has evolved as education over that time to where we are now? What do we now accept so much as fact that it is hard to believe things were ever different? Schools have come to be positioned as institutions that authenticate particular forms of knowledge and skills and favour certain ways rather than others and seek to have these taken up by their charges, children. The manner in which this has developed has meant the construction of schools as more analogous to a factory than to a garden or an art studio. The standards agenda dominates schools today, with high penalties for those who cannot produce outcomes in terms of percentages of children achieving five or more grads A to C at GCSE. There is little room for different terrains where diversity can grow.

Whilst more imaginative teaching may produce the creative thinkers who can pass any exam, the safest way to achieve higher results is to concentrate on the tests, and teach for the test. This has led therefore to a predominance in schools of the transmission view of education, that there is 'an objective world of meaning and facts that the developing pupil needs to absorb ... [pupils] should learn these facts and procedures precisely in the way that they are represented in the subject-matter, the curriculum documents' (Wardekker and Miedema, 2001: 78). This can be contrasted with a view of education as transformation, that is, not the 'transmission of the teachable content or subject matter, of knowledge, skills, values and norms, but rather the transformation of these into a heuristic base for acting' (Wardekker and Miedema, 2001: 80).

The most powerful discourses are often those least readily available, as they are so much assumed, like part of the wallpaper. Coming into this category is the ambivalence that exists in schools about change, and particularly the influence teachers have over any change and development that might be seen in individual children and young people. An experienced colleague, a professional who offers advice to schools, recently told me that one of the most effective influences on teachers that he has ever seen has been a recent phenomenon, and is Black's 'black box' (Black and Williams, 1998), an approach to formative assessment. This has, he claimed, enabled teachers to experience the effects of their teaching and to see that children do indeed learn – that they, as teachers do have an effect. The counter-perspective to this is that children and young people have relatively fixed identities as 'learning receptacles' such that some will take in lots of knowledge (these understood as 'bright' or 'able' children) and others only have a capacity for a little (those of 'low ability'), and that the role of the schools is to fill these receptacles with whatever amount of curriculum is appropriate for the 'different types of learners'. These assumptions interact with others, discussed in the next sections, about people and context.

Schools can be seen as 'arenas in which the tension and conflicts of social division are of central importance' (Wilson and Wyn, 1993: 6) where embattled teachers and other professionals must defend their professionalism and sometimes do so by erecting barriers between themselves and parents (Hannon, 1995). For example:

> The Head's and the class teacher's insistence on a behavioural label and refusal to accept a learning difficulty or to relate his difficulties to his 'ability', can be seen as an attempt to maintain their professional identity.
>
> (Armstrong *et al.*, 1993: 400)

> Teachers can maintain their sense of themselves as skilled professionals if they are able to have challenging pupils legitimately identified as the responsibility of others and if they can 'redefine their role in terms of the skills associated with teaching "normal" children'.
>
> (Todd and Higgins, 1998: 234, quoting Armstrong, 1993)

The discourses of practice in schools that construct how we think of learning but also support norms and labels are ones that seem unlikely to encourage participation with either children or parents. An example of alternative practices of teaching and learning can be found in Chapter 7 in one of the case studies of inclusive collaborative practice, looking at democratic RE (Baumfield, 2003).

Concluding thoughts

The assumption of a monopoly of expertise infuses all practice whether this is actually upheld or not by any individual practitioner in schools and services. When this teams up with a transmission view of education and the idea that we can have very little influence over children/young people, it is hard to see how inclusive education, assuming our broad and critical definition, will ever have its day. What is needed is first and foremost a critical approach to how we are as teachers, mentors, doctors, psychologists etc. – to render the impact of our assumptions visible. Then, we need a way of teaching and of delivering services that challenges some of the assumptions of practice that mitigate against participation, in order to allow other knowledges, other understandings of teaching and learning, other stories of identity to be in evidence and play an active role in schools and services. This requires further understandings – about people and about context – to which we turn next.

People: the assumptions we have of the children and families with whom we work

The assumptions made about people – about what a parent is and about how we understand childhood – all help to form the way we work in schools and in child or family-focused services. These are summarised in Table 6.2. Some support participation, others make participation more difficult. This has been a recurring theme throughout the book. Models of the child as in need of our protection, as immature and unreliable self-advocates, or as easily likely to behave in ways unacceptable to adults have all assisted in providing reasons for professionals to hesitate before involving children in decision-making (Chapters 2 and 3). The pervading image of parenthood as lacking competence, and a history of seeing parents as part of the problem when their children experience difficulties at school have detracted from any kind of equality or reciprocity in their relationships with professionals (Chapter 4). What can be seen throughout the discussions in these chapters is a catalogue of 'thin' descriptions, thin conclusions, about the parents and children with whom we work. These thin conclusions

Table 6.2 The implications for partnership of alternative assumptions about People

Conceptualisations of People

Against partnership	For partnership
Thin descriptions and thin conclusions about children, young people and parents.	Rich descriptions of lives and relationships.
Certain models of childhood: innocent to be protected, wild beast to be tamed.	Certain models of childhood: possesses own perspectives and abilities to express perspectives, makes active sense of self and happenings.
Children and parents believed lacking in competence.	Children and parents believed to possess competence. People have expertise, knowledges and skills to solve their own problems.
Deficit and blame discourse of parents and young people.	Blame and deficit notions replaced by different understandings of context.
An assumption that the person is the problem.	An assumption that the person is not the problem: the problem is the problem. Human rights claims for children and parents.

become reproduced in the context of some discourses of professional practice, when an already thin image becomes fixed (Chapter 5). More expanded ideas, historical, sociological and political, about how we understand the child and the family can be found in a number of texts (Prout, 2005; James and Prout, 1990; Chambers, 2001; Edwards, 2002; Hallett and Prout, 2003; Hudak and Kihn, 2001; Wyness, 2000).

What is argued is the need for rich descriptions of lives and relationships. Thin conclusions of children and parents – how they might become known to schools and services – may not sufficiently represent their lived experience. Access only to thin conclusions suggests an inadequate basis for relationships and decisions. Access to a rich story of parents in Chapter 4 led to the suggestion that it is the school rather than the parents that may be hard to reach. We have seen evidence of the ability of children and young people to articulate what they want in schools and services (Chapter 2). When children's rich stories of their experiences of services were available (in Chapter 3) we were able to start to understand what is getting in the way of child involvement in decision-making.

It is the thin conclusions of children and parents that are most readily available and that arise from how we currently function in schools and services. They arise from discourses of people and context. The authority for more rich descriptions and stories of people's lives are the people themselves – the children, young people and parents. If we accept an understanding of *children* and *parents* as 'multi-storied' and as 'holding expertise over their own lives', there emerges a pressing need for collaborative relationships as practitioners no longer hold the most important knowledge. However, practices *are* available that are consistent with this thinking. Solution-focused thinking assumes people have within themselves the skills to solve their problems (Rhodes and Ajmal, 1995). Narrative practices look to enable the telling of rich rather than thin stories of people's lives, and understands lived experience as expertise (O'Neill and Stockell, 2003). More about both approaches can be found in Chapter 7. Furthermore, there is some awareness now in the research literature on multi-agency working of the 'capacity of service users and their families to help tailor the services they are receiving' (Edwards, 2005: 6) and talk of ' "client-led" interagency collaboration' (Edwards, 2005: 12).

It follows that we may need a different way of thinking about the knowledge of children and parents, and therefore of professionals. The duality contrasting expert knowledge/objective with personal/subjective seems no longer appropriate. 'Personal' is insufficient as a descriptor of the intense and vivid stories of live and relationships. But also, professionals are people – and parents too – and have their own rich stories. 'Professionals are constantly evolving and "becoming" too' (Goodley *et al.*, 2006: 4). Assumptions about 'personal' knowledge as distinct from professional may not be valid. Parent competence is discounted and invisible in relation to that of the professional (see Chapter 4). Commonly occurring ideas about the personal is that it is self-interested and self-serving, or biased, and can therefore be discounted: 'I would say [parents know] probably a hell of a lot, actually. It's their child. But they're going to be biased, aren't they?' (clinical psychologist) (Todd, 2000a).

There seems to be a richer description of the personal that would challenge such silencing, and these are supported by ideas from narrative practices (Chapter 7). Vincent and Martin (2000: 476) carried out research into discussion-based parents' forums at two secondary schools. They critique their own observation that parents attend one group to maximise the educational outcome for their own child(ren) by acknowledging the particular and the private as a legitimate motivation for participation.

> Suppressing particularity, rendering individual concerns invalid, will . . . detract from people's willingness to participate. . . . Self-interest is incomplete as an explanation for participation, that there are other elements at play here or to be more precise, self-interest can be more widely conceived.
>
> (Vincent and Martin, 2000: 476)

> when people think about what they want, they think about more than just their narrow self interest. When they define their own interests and when they act to pursue those interests, they often give great weight both to their moral principles and to the interests of others.
>
> (Vincent and Martin, 2000: 476)

The discovery of people's purposes, intentions and values for their lives is part of the development, in narrative practices, of preferred identities. This is the case whether working with children experiencing a problem at school or with a multi-professional team looking to develop ways to work together. Old dichotomomies between the expertise of the professional and the subjective of the child/parent disappear when we are concerned with hopes, purposes and values, as we are all our own experts in what is important to us. The personal becomes – indeed is – professional and vice versa. The roles of the parents, child and professional in their collaborations need different kinds of thinking: old models have had their day.

There needs to be further debate on the importance of the personal and the subjective. In Chapter 5, a recognition of the individual – without individualisation – was crucial for the parents involved in an exclusion project in primary schools. Parents of children with special needs and disabilities say one of the most important aspects of any professional engagement is that the professional should see their child as an individual, as a person. This was of such importance in Goodley and McLaughlin *et al.*'s research with parents of very young children with disabilities that a key finding was that 'just one committed professional can make all the difference to the lives of children and their families' (Goodley *et al.*, 2006: 5).

As the author was nearing the completion of this book, she was rather perturbed that the section on people seemed fairly slim. However, in many ways this *is* all there is to say about people as what we really want is for practice to develop so that people – parents, children/ young people, workers – get a chance to express themselves. Also, much of what we could say about people is by way of caution and comes into other chapters of the book and other sections of this chapter, particularly pp. 117–119 looking at professional practice as fixing the image of a person, and p. 127, warning of the discourses of norms and labels that calls us into seeing people according to narrow identity conclusions.

Context: the meaning given to the context

How we understand context, 'the environment', and what we believe about the relationship we and those with whom we work have with 'context' is crucial to how we work with people. Why is this? Many of the problems that have been discussed in this book in developing partnership working can be understood as a failure to understand the relationship between the individual, practice and context. A failure either to understand the implications of the context of our own professional working for the kind of practice that is possible, or a failure to understand the people with whom we work are themselves functioning within a context. Some assumptions of context that have different implications for partnership are summarised in Table 6.3. Some of these are further expanded in the following text.

Cultural, economic and political contexts

The educational failure and exclusion of children and young people living in disadvantaged areas are believed to have complex origins requiring joined-up solutions that tackle related problems of unemployment, chronic health problems, high crime rates, and other social problems. Theories of economic, social and cultural capital are often drawn upon both to explain the continuing nature of disadvantage as well as to propose ways forward. Blame theory and deficit notions of parents often fail to take fully into consideration such endemic contextual problems. However, even when context is recognised, this can confirm problem identities. More recent research has sought to make known the cultural capital that exists in areas of disadvantage (Seaman and Sweeting, 2004). Others have shown how economic considerations (Vincent, 2000) and the impact of gender (David, 1993) and ethnicity (Crozier and Davies, 2007) are often ignored in home–school relations. The impact of the inner-city context

Table 6.3 The implications for partnership of alternative assumptions about Context

Relationship with Context

Against partnership	*For partnership*
Understanding of context as a separate influence on the individual.	Understanding of individual as inseparable from context.
Lack of adequate awareness of cultural, organisational and political influences.	Willingness to examine and act in relation to cultural, organisational and political influences.
Discourse of professional independence – a lack of recognition that professional systems assist in creating identities.	Acceptance that professional practice is part of the context within which identities (both problem and solution identities) are created. Willingness to examine and make visible social practices.
Acceptance of norms.	Challenging norms

on children is highlighted by parents (Fox, 2004). The move to develop the role of the educational psychologist as a community psychologist is a recognition of the need to work with people in the context of their communities (King and Wilson, 2006; MacKay, 2006). Current reorganisations of services according to a broad social inclusion agenda represent a powerful statement about the importance of the social, political, economic and historical context, and is dealt with to some detail in Chapter 5.

The professional cannot be understood separate of context

The understanding of the professional as 'independent', one of the key discourses of practice, means it is difficult to see ourselves as part of the context that constructs children and parents. Post-structuralist ideas presented in Chapter 1 suggest it is part of being human that we both shape society and are shaped by it – and this is no less true in professional practice than in other areas of life. So, we cannot be seen as independent actors, exerting the benign good of our professional tools on those in need of our skills. We exert tools, but we are of part of some separate context. It is suggested that the professional plays a role, through the different frameworks and agendas, in shaping the identity possibilities of those with whom we work (see also pp. 117–119):

professionals are more like artists than scientists, fashioning identities from their particular professional perspectives. Professionals
can be understood as all operating through different frame-works,
using different ways of seeing. What is found by chiselling at clay
is different according to who is doing the chiselling, what tools are
used, and how the artist goes about the task. This constructing is a
power. When all you have is a hammer.

(Todd, 2006)

The context in terms of societally imposed norms

Context can also be understood in terms of culturally constructed
norms that call us into seeing people as categories rather than the rich
diversity of their own identities. Research has found that, for example,
children and young people who have a disability have ambivalent relationships with an identity as 'disabled' (Allen, 1999; Watson *et al.*,
1999). Sometimes they want to be seen as someone with a disability
and at other times they want to be seen as any other child or young
person, as someone with the same interests, fears and hopes as others.
However, they find that the systems of schools and services, and the
attitudes they come across, mean they are more often than not seen in
terms of categories and labels. Other norms are similarly imposed in
the context of schools as there is 'pressure from . . . peers and teachers
to conform into narrowly defined gender roles and sexualities', a
pressure towards compulsory heterosexuality. For the most part, the
validity of homosexual/lesbian/bisexual identity is simply ignored,
or treated more as an illness (Ellis and High, 2004: 221), which also
means that homosexual bullying is not dealt with (Harris, 2000;
Mac an Ghaill, 1994). Crozier (2005: 596) suggests there is a 'pathological view of the black, or in this case Afrocaribbean child, that is so
embedded with the school institution that conspires against his or her
success'. Phillips (2003) deconstructs the language of prejudice for a
child looked after by the local authority. The understanding of inclusive education assumed in this book (Chapter 1) requires the challenging of such norms. Collaborative working similarly requires an
engagement with people on their own terms rather than in terms of
constructed identities. And it is only with this collaboration that we
will develop the richer stories of people's lived experience that will
challenge such narrow identity conclusions (see also pp. 121–125).

The organisational context

There is a level of authority that can play a defining role in how we carry out what we do when we try to enable children or parents to have a greater role in decision-making. These are organisational and institutional demands. Such demands can be found whatever the organisation, the school, the PCT, the LA, or individual agencies. These dictates are numerous and change frequently in the current culture of reorganisation and bureaucratic approaches to quality assurance. Examples of key organisational pressures that operate in institutions:

- standards agenda . . . SATs and their use in a school;
- Ofsted, other inspection frameworks for social services etc.;
- service reorganisation – integrated services;
- becoming a specialist school, an extended school, a dyslexic friendly school etc.;
- targets: assessment time limits, per cent passes at different exam grades, criteria for professional involvement.

These demands call us into acting in particular ways as a response. They can provide a range of managerial preoccupations that can become the drivers of our practice, rather than practice being driven by our own values and purposes for our work. 'Parents and professionals are caught up in the privatisation and marketisation of health, social care and education' (Goodley *et al.*, 2006: 5).

Concern for academic standards, with a direct link to inspection mechanisms, can play a predominant role in the kinds of practices in teaching and learning that are possible. In services there are similar targets, many in terms of the time for professionals to respond to various demands and to cope with shortage of professional staff, or the 'level of difficulty' required before a response from a professional is triggered. It can be difficult for professionals to carve time, for example, for collaborative group work with parents, if there are organisational targets to be hit. Professionals attending a meeting to look at ways to meet the needs of children causing concern can find their roles already defined by their institution, inhibiting creative solutions for children. Indeed, often the stress in trying to meet institutional demands is such that, far from finding solutions, a predominant professional concern is more the avoidance of 'taking on' any further 'cases'. If there are institutional rules about what needs to be found in a child's situation in order to enable professional involvement or in order to allow the provision of resources in school, this gives little reason to negotiate professional involvement directly with the child. Similarly, the context within which letters are written to children – and reports are written about them – may be very prescribed by rules about what an assessment consists of. These and much more besides create a managerial context driving professional practice. They are strong powerful drivers that often leave little room for the collaborative engagement with clients.

The need for a more mature understand of context

What seems to happen in schools and services is a lip-service to context. We verbally acknowledge the 'environment', a child's background, i.e. unemployment in the area as part of the story explaining the situations that present themselves in the classroom or the consulting room. But most of the actions available to us assume the 'problem' lies 'within' the child or adult with whom we are working – so our actions support this. The constructed nature of professional practice – and therefore its political nature – seems rarely acknowledged.

It may be helpful if further thinking happened about what context actually is. A central issue for psychology (as also referred to in Chapter 5) has been resolving the relationship between the individual and culture and society – or the context. Are problems internal to the person, and does the context in which the person lives provide several additional influences on the problem, or is the context part of the creation of the problem? Does thought develop internally and then become shared with others socially, so brought into the context – or is thought developed first socially? Should teachers consider the home background as a variable having a main impact on a child's motivation to learn, or is the school itself part of the context that, together with home, community and all aspects of cultural life, construct the learning identities of children? There follow some theoretical considerations to assist in thinking about these questions.

The approach taken by this book, consistent with community psychology (Kagan *et al.*, 2006), is one based on ideas from sociocultural psychology and social constructionism/post-structuralism. We cannot understand practice – or any human thoughts, feelings or actions – separate from context. Often, we speak of 'the environment' as something that is separate from the individual but has an effect on our actions. That is not the way that context is being used here. Here it is being suggested that context is not something that surrounds, has an influence, is outside, but it is, to take Cole's definition, 'that which weaves together' (Cole, 1996: 135): the connected whole that gives coherence to its parts. A helpful image is provided from the study of language:

> a phoneme exists only in combination with other phonemes which make up a word. The word is the context of the phoneme. But the word exists as such – 'has meaning' – only in a relationship to a larger unit of discourse.
>
> (Cole, 1996: 134)

We assist in the creation of context, and at the same time our actions, feelings and thoughts are subject to the context, as we interpret them in terms of the context, and as they arise from the context. Bourdieu (1977), according to Cole (1996), resists simplified ideas of context as cause, or dualistic theories of cognition and social life through his notion of *habitus*, as 'a system of lasting, transposable dispositions which, integrating past experiences, functions at every moment as a matrix of perceptions, appreciations, and actions and makes possible the achievement of infinitely diversified tasks' (Bourdieu, 1977: 82–83). It is 'history made nature . . . the (usually) unexamined, background set of assumptions about the world' (Bourdieu, 1977: 78). The important point here is that *habitus* is so much part of our lives that we almost do not realise it is there. It is the taken for granted. In the context of this book, it is the aspects of professional role that we step into without realising as they are always there. Included here are the assumptions already spoken of, including neutrality, objectivity, independence, and the 'unquestioned-ness' of what we do.

Following on from the quote from Bourdieu is a further important idea to add to the thinking in this book; it is that today is (partially) formed by yesterday: 'the activities of human beings, at all stages of development and organization, are social products and must be seen as historical developments' (Holzman, 1996).

To recap, we have argued, in different ways, for the inseparability of the individual and society – culture – the context; in a context we take for granted, and one that has evolved historically. But we still need some way of understanding how we can think of ourselves within the context – how can we understand the problems of professionals, parents and children if they are all part of some great amorphous context? Is there no way to think of the constituent parts of context but at the same time maintain an understanding of them as inseparable? If we can do this, what are the 'parts' – the ideas and concepts – that would assist in thinking about partnerships in inclusive education? Different traditions of thought, of cultural theory and of psychology have come up with different ways to do this, and each has a different contribution. Psychology gives us ideas that look at human actions in terms of 'activity', action mediated by tools and artefacts. Socio-cultural historical activity theorists, developing ideas from Vygotsky and Luria, understand context as relational, as activity systems – as different components that do not exist in isolation from one another, and are 'constantly being constructed, renewed and transformed as outcome and cause of human life' (Cole, 1996: 141). We have already seen these ideas demonstrated as practical theories – via activity systems (Engestrom, 1996; Engestrom *et al.*, 1999) – in exploring multi-agency working (Chapter 5).

Another way that context avoids being some kind of deterministic all-encompassing swamp swallowing the individual draws on ideas from social constructionism. These assist us to understand something important about power, and to see how some knowledges become privileged, whilst others are discredited (see pp. 117–119, 121–125 and 127). We are subject to power, not a hierarchical power, but a constitutive power (Foucault, 1979; Foucault, 1980; Foucault, 1984; White and Epston, 1990). This happens through the normalising 'truths' that shape our lives (White and Epston, 1990: 19):

> We are all caught up in a net or web of power/knowledge, it is not possible to act apart from this domain and we are simultaneously undergoing the effects of power and exercising this power in relation to others. However, this does not, by any means suggest that all persons are equal in the exercise of power, nor that some do not suffer its subjugating effects very much more than others.
>
> (White and Epston, 1990: 22)

The ascendancy of certain knowledges (i.e. scientific knowledge, the expertise of the professional) over others means that other alternative knowledges are disqualified, and people or groups (in this book, those of parents and children) are diminished (White and Epston, 1990). The latter includes 'erudite' knowledges, such as those made available by feminist writing and struggle. They also include 'local popular', 'indigenous', 'regional', 'popular' knowledges, and 'folk psychologies'. These include notions about our beliefs, values, actions and relationships that are known in communities but not validated by science or other regimes of power. More on folk psychologies can be found in White (2004).

Once again, it is not that people are subjugated by other people in a hierarchical sense. It is that their knowledges are disqualified, but also that people are recruited into an active role in their own subjugation. We perpetually evaluate our own behaviour according to accepted societal norms, 'this is the society of the everpresent "gaze" ' (White and Epston, 1990: 23). Professional knowledge and thin conclusions of people and communities are privileged. In the subjugation of people's richly storied lives and their folk psychologies/local knowledges, it is not simply a case of professionals refusing to listen, but a cultural disposition not to notice these alternative stories, psychologies and knowledges. As a professional, speaking to my child's teacher about a concern I have, I am as nervous as any parent, assuming the role of submissive parent to the more knowing professional. No-one needs to silence me: I silence myself.

However, this power is not invisible, its effects can be seen and norms can be open to critique. The other knowledges can be resurrected and made visible. What this book has all been about, and it is the central purpose of the PPC Model, is the process of making this happen. Chapter 7 looks more explicitly at some various and alternative ways for making spaces in practice to allow alternative knowledges and rich stories. This is, the author argues, what is required for collaborative practice to take place.

Conclusion

Partnership may have had its day. Maybe it has never existed. There has been much rhetoric about listening, and about partnership being one of equal but different expertise. Such ideas by themselves without a consideration of all aspects of the PPC Model – in particular the aspect of critical practice – have been found wanting. The PPC Model also avoids any simplistic calls to 'empower' parents and children. Figure 6.1 shows the elements of the PPC Model of professional working that contribute to authentic collaborative working relationships – in schools and services – with children, young people and parents. We have seen, in Chapter 5, how different ways of constructing multi-agency meetings were able in different ways to follow some of these approaches and assumptions but not others, and to very different outcomes. We are perhaps at the start of an exploration of ways to work together with other professionals to structure interactions between ourselves and parents and children in very different ways.

The first requirement is to challenge practices that go against our own values and motives for our work first by starting to understand professional practice, whether of teachers or others, as 'politics'. We can, again drawing on White and Epston (1990) try to establish conditions that help us to critique our own practices, and part of this would involve joining with others to assist us:

> [We can] work to identify the context of ideas in which our practices are situated and explore the history of these ideas. This would enable us to identify more readily the effects, dangers, and limitations of these ideas and of our own practices . . . we would work to identify and critique those aspects of our work that might relate to the techniques of social control.
>
> (White and Epston, 1990: 29)

Part of this task will be a careful look at the language we use, as the terms of professional practice play an active role in the construction of professional practice and, therefore, in the construction of identities of parents and children. Phillips (2003) offers a model to show how we might go about looking at social and cultural practices in her deconstruction of the 'language of prejudice' for a child in public care. Narrative practices are about working collaboratively with people in a deconstructive way, deconstructing language, problems and context (see Chapter 7).

There is no shortage of calls to re-negotiate our relationship with our own practice and with the children and adults with whom we work in order to develop a more inclusive society – with more inclusive schools. Statham (2000) sees the need for a profound cultural change, towards recognising a social model of disability, racial and cultural diversity and social inclusion – all of which are based upon civil rights and removing barriers and discrimination. Roffey (2004) talks in terms of professionals having to co-construct reality with parents. Skrtic argues for 'critical pragmatism' when working with families, or the practice of 'approaching decision-making in a way that recognises and treats as problematic the assumptions, theories, and meta theories behind professional models, practice, and tools' (Skrtic, 1995: 44). Statham sees this cultural change as placing people using services in an entirely different relationship with professionals, developing within professionals the capacity to operate across the boundaries of professions and systems. A change from patronage to partnership is seen to be possible, but only within a time-scale of some ten years (Statham, 2000: 89). Statham's revisioning of partnership seem consonant with Galloway's 'democratic professionalism' (Galloway *et al.*, 1994: 129) or Vincent and Warren's (1997) call for different way of relating (to parents) to be explored that achieve different outcomes. Allen (1999: 119) suggests 'refusing the other', refusing to gaze, and allowing the 'cannibal desire to know the other give way to the act of hearing what the speaker says'. Professionals should refuse to offer promises of rescue or escape routes to the 'grounds of certainty'. Professionals should recognise the way inclusion has been fictionalised. Many authors have looked to the creation of services wanted by the people who use them. Allen looks to the creation of spaces for dialogue and boundary crossing – but acknowledges that these spaces can also be oppressive. Professionals may need to start to uncover the personal, subjective and affective. In the process, they may find themselves challenging their own 'Professional Thought Disorder' (PTD):

> a compulsion to analyse and categorise the experience of others, disordered cognition – rigidly held beliefs, delusions of grandeur, negative transference and projection in which sufferers cannot distinguish their own wishes and impulses from those of the people they wish to be helping.
>
> (Defined by Allen, 1999: 119)

Billington *et al.* (2000) critique assessment that employs deficit models based on broad categories and are based on assumptions. They argue instead to see individuals, start from listening to parents and children and teachers, and to connect assessments with what actually happens in schools. Practice should look for abilities and conduct 'assessments as relationships ... information in which a child's performance can be seen as less isolated from their environmental circumstances' (Billington *et al.*, 2000: 66).

Kalyanpur *et al.* (2000) go further than this, and perhaps comes closest to the practice embodied in the model (Figure 6.2), arguing strongly for a need to develop 'cultural reciprocity' with those with whom we work (families and children) via 'explicit discussions with families'. The way to develop this is through a relationship: 'a process that evolves much like a friendship: using conversation and mutual self-disclosure, avoiding formal measures of any kind, and proceeding at a pace that is unhurried and with an attitude that is non-judgemental, supportive, and caring' (Kalyanpur *et al.*, 2000: 132). There is an incumbent need to 'respect the new bodies of knowledge that emerges from these discussions, and make allowances for differences in perspective when responding to the family's need'.

With national reorganisations of services for children and the continuation of initiatives such as Sure Start and extended schools, there are some exciting opportunities to re-negotiate the ways schools and services engage in order to facilitate more inclusion. However, there is also a real danger that this moment will not be grasped, in the sheer volume of changes and pressures and in the very weight of restricting and oppressive discourses.

7 Towards authentic participation

Examples of practice

Introduction

This book began asking how real, authentic partnership could be developed between children and young people, parents and practitioners in order to facilitate inclusive education. Throughout the book it has been argued that we need to concentrate on participation, on collaboration, in order for inclusive education to be furthered. This is not to ignore the existence of a range of relationships between professionals and clients. It is also not to ignore many other areas important for the development of inclusive education such as resources and curriculum. Such areas are beyond the scope of this book. But also, the definition of inclusive education that has been adopted in every chapter is one that puts collaboration as central to what inclusion is about. It is precisely this collaboration that seems elusive. It is that we are looking for a relationship that gives agency and power to those whom practitioners teach and are consulted by – and this agency, for children and parents, seems so hard to achieve. It is not as if the notion of partnership is novel, as it has become increasingly prominent in the policy documents relating to health, education and social services, and in particular in those relating to inclusive education. The notion is not novel – but we still do not seem to understand what it is or how to go about achieving it to any widespread degree. 'Partnership' runs through the development of children's services. It seems important on many counts therefore to make sure that it is happening in more than lip-service.

Chapter 6 summarised the understandings and theoretical underpinnings of previous chapters. It introduced and developed the PPC Model, a framework or map to help navigate professional practice towards participation. There is merit in returning to Figure 6.1, to the key elements from this model that contribute to collaborative relationships in schools and services:

1. *A critical approach*: a willingness is needed to recognise how the discourses of professional practice shape relationships between professionals and children and parents and therefore the identity options for children, parents and professionals. Willingness to examine context in its various guises – to make visible social practices and to examine cultural, organisational and political influences.

2. *A de-centred relationship* with children and parents is required that recognises them as holding expertise over their lives and finds ways to bring to the fore the rich variety in lived experience, of community, relationships and learning.

3. *Keeping problems in their place* should be central priority, so that people – children, young people and adults – are not viewed in terms of their problems. The problem is the problem.

4. *The agent of change is communal*: practices need to be found in the different contexts in which we work – in classes, in group-work with young people and parents, in meetings, and in individual sessions with children and adults, in teaching, mentoring, coaching, medical consultations, counselling – that create 'spaces'. These are opportunities for different knowledges to be heard and to have influence.

In this chapter, a range of current activities that in different ways and to different degreees exemplify the PPC Model of collaborative practice (Figure 6.1) are described. Firstly, two different 'movements' in practice are briefly summarised. These are 'narrative practices' and 'solution-orientated approaches'. Both resonate well with the PPC Model. Collaboration and participation is central to each, as is an active appreciation of people's knowledges of life. Whilst both start from being an approach to therapy, these movements find application at a number of levels (individual, group, organisation, community) and in all disciplines (education, mental health, health, social care, industry etc.). They are outlined next, together with key references to find out more, before presenting four case studies from other developments in work with children and families that give strong evidence – or potential – of collaboration.

The case study examples include the following:

- Case 1: Transforming learning in schools – Democratic RE

- Case 2: Involving children and young people in decision-making in the development of services – 'Investing in Children'
- Case 3: Family Group Conferences
- Case 4: Extended Schools

The need, clearly articulated in this book, for a critical approach to professional practice might give the impression that no-one is succeeding in collaborative practice. This is not at all the case. There are numerous creative projects and pieces of work in schools and services that evidence collaborative inclusive practice consistent with the PPC Model. But it is not widespread and there are clearly difficulties. There are a large number of other initiatives and projects that could have found their way into case studies.

Case 1 was selected to demonstrate how a collaboration between researchers and teachers that gave attention to the teaching and learning in the classroom was able to develop a better sense of collaboration in learning between teachers and pupils (Baumfield, 2003; Baumfield, 2002). The pivot was the use of an approach to thinking skills, 'Philosophy for Children'. In keeping with the assumption in this book of the inseparable relationship between inclusive education and collaboration, this example shows children more included in the classroom as effective learners.

Case 2 is a very different example of inclusive practice with children and young people. It goes to the heart of much of the discussion from Chapters 2 and 3, and describes the work of an agency, 'Investing in Children', where children and young people, as researchers and consultants, play a leading role in the development of services (Cairns, 2001).

Case 3 is an example of collaboration within families and between families and professionals in the Family Group Conference. These are found both nationally and internationally, and seek to involve family members in solving problems that involve child welfare or protection issues.

Finally, Case 4 is an example of a more all-embracing initiative that has been gaining ground for a while in the UK and internationally (Cummings *et al.*, 2005; Cummings *et al.*, 2004; Sammons *et al.*, 2003). Extended schooling aims for greater collaboration between schools and other agencies and professionals to more effectively meet the needs of communities. There is a broad aim of social inclusion. There are encouraging initial outcomes. However, one of the questions for extended schools is what kinds of collaboration they can develop with children, families and others in the school communities.

Finally, the Appendix lists ideas from research of children and young people about the services they might want.

Narrative practices

Narrative practices that professionals can use in schools, with individuals and in meetings with children and in team meetings with other professionals, are all, in effect, about the development of collaborative inclusive practice (Smith and Nylund, 1997; White and Epston, 1990; Winslade and Monk, 1999). They are highly resonant with the model discussed in Chapter 6, and summarised above. Narrative practices are used in therapy, but they have also been applied to many different kinds of situations, including working with groups in schools and communities.

Taking life into story lines

According to narrative understandings, we are routinely involved in the making of meaning. We give meaning to our experiences of life by taking them into a story line. Making meaning is an achievement and gives shape to our lives. The cultural and political context, with messages about, for example, gender, race, class, sexuality and disability, are powerful influences on the sense we make of our experiences. We are also highly selective about what we attribute meaning to: it is impossible to give meaning to everything. Many aspects of lived experience stand outside these story lines. There is therefore a huge stock of neglected lived experiences we can draw on.

Externalising

Narrative conversations assist people to break from thin conclusions about their lives and thin descriptions by which they know themselves. It presents options, for example, for people to become other than who they are when their way of knowing themselves is problem dominated (O'Neill and Stockell, 2003). Questions are asked not to gather information but to generate the experience of preferred realities. Questions provide linguistic resources – offer possible ways to think about a situation. Externalising is the practice of understanding and talking about problems as separate from people. Externalising conversations place problems into a story line to shed light on how the problem has come to have such an influence on someone's life and also to provide people with information and understanding about how they can reclaim their lives from the influence of the problem (Russell and Carey, 2004). This is not the same thing as encouraging people to tell a different story, to replace a problem story with a different perspective. By externalising the problem it becomes possible for the person to investigate their relationship with the problem and to take responsibility for revising that relationship. It can be useful to explore with someone their experience of life, of how the problem affects their life, and of the influence of the person on the problem. There may be a conversation to find a name for the problem that reflects the person's experience. Exploring the effects of problems and situating these effects in the broader social context allows for their deconstruction. The conversations also take account of the ways people's relationships with problems are shaped by history and culture, and explore how gender, race, culture, sexuality, class and other relations of power have influenced the construction of the problem (Russell and Carey, 2004: 5).

Unique outcomes – preferred stories

During conversations the therapist is on the look-out for unique outcomes (sparkling moments): for anything that contradicts the problem-saturate story, an exception to the dominant plot. Therapists listen doubly, for the absent but implicit. In the description of a problem by someone is always (perhaps unspoken) reference to their resistance to it. These provide entry-points to the development of an alternative or preferred story. There is a conversation that encourages curiosity about unique outcomes and about whether they have a history in someone's life so that unique events are richly described. As a guide to re-authored conversations, Michael White has developed maps that ask 'landscape of identity' questions and 'landscape of action questions'. These create a story line for alternative identities based on the events, 'landscape of action', in people's lives and the meaning, 'landscape of identity', people give these events for their lives. When therapists hear unique outcomes it is important that they do not try to convince the client of the significance of these outcomes – that they do not lead on their own understanding of the meaning of these events. We invite people to make meaning out of events that have been neglected. In this way there is an unstalling the initiatives of life, whose effect is often disqualified or ridiculed, to enable instead these iniatives to have an enduring effect.

Thickening the preferred story

There are a number of other ways to richly describe the preferred story. One is through remembering conversations which evoke the views and perspectives of people who can contribute to the further development of the story. A client might be asked if there is someone who would recognise or appreciate a development, an initiative, in someone's life that has been spoken about in the narrative conversation – and the new story of identity is linked to the story of the lives of other people. Another way of involving other people in the process of thickening preferred stories is through the use of outsider witness for the therapy conversations (Russell and Carey, 2004). The outsider witness can be family, friends or other people. Having someone witness therapy conversations and respond (in ways structured carefully by the therapist) can be very significant for the client. It can thicken the preferred stories in very important ways, can reduce the feeling of isolation that often results from a problem. It can be very creative. Links are made in the stories of the life of the client with those in the lives of the outsider witness group (Russell and Carey, 2004).

Professional roles – decentred – influential

The influence of the professional is in terms of how he or she positions themselves in the relationship with the people with whom they are working. It is in terms of asking questions in certain ways consistent with this positioning. The position is 'non-expert influential' that holds the ideas and resources of the person at the fore:

> [this position] does not need to imply that we give up our authority as professionals. We do not withdraw completely from the authoring role in counselling relationships. But we do endeavour to use our authority in ways that put our weight behind that client's preference for agency in his own life. We do this by deliberately choosing what we give attention to and how we align ourselves. The narrative alignment is against problems, against isolating, deficit-inducing discourses, and for people.
>
> (Monk *et al.*, 1996: 61)

We may be working with people who are not routinely in the territory of language. If this is the case, it is important that we take responsibility for the person not to experience, from our conversations with them, a failure to know.

Using narrative practices to address bullying in a classroom

Alice Morgan reports on her use of narrative practices with bullying in a classroom between girls (Morgan, 1995: 19). She wanted to find a way of working without contributing to or reproducing structuralist discourses. The latter involved blame in different ways (the teacher for not doing enough to deal with the problem or the parents for not providing an adequate upbringing). Structuralist solutions also emphasise the need to look for causes to explain the bullies' behaviour, or for a view of victims as pathological in some way (i.e. the cause being not enough of certain skills or characteristics).

Alice Morgan instead saw parallels with racism, and wanted to tackle the classroom bullying in terms of the abuse of power of a dominant group against a marginalised group. She wanted those in the dominant group to take full responsibility for changing their own repressive behaviour. Morgan expresses the idea that to ask the victims of the abuse to articulate the effects of the abuse would be to further burden them (Morgan, 1995). She wanted the girls who had per-petrated the abuse to 'get together and speak in their own voices against the abuse' (Morgan, 1995: 19). Her main assumption was that only the abusive person can change his/her beliefs and behaviours.

Morgan explored with the girls what kind of teasing happened, and the effects of teasing on their experience of school and on their rela-tionships within the class. This exploration took place over several group sessions and became a project which the girls worked on with imagination and enthusiasm. Alice Morgan asked narrative questions that were in the context of her relationship with the girls. A number of things emerged in more richly describing the effects of the problem and the positions taken by the girls on these effects. One aspect was that 'teams' were formed in the class by powerful class members who recruited others usually through bribery. On investigating this aspect of their experience of the class, they decided they unanimously hated 'teams'. Alice Morgan externalised 'teams' to find out the effect of them on the girls lives. One session the girls told Alice that there had been no teams the previous week, and this led to a discussion about how they had managed that, what personal qualities they had used, and who else would have noticed. This is an example of a collabor-ation between a practitioner and children in which children's know-ledges were the agent of change. The practitioner took a critical approach to existing understandings about bullying and a de-centred role in working with the children.

Other ways narrative practices are used

- Outsider witness practices can be used in team development in multi-agency services, and where a group of workers are experiencing difficulties. The different conversations that happen can enable professionals to get to know more about the 'hope, commitments, intentions and histories' of each other in new ways (Russell and Carey, 2004: 85).
- Narrative practices can be used in lots of different ways to work with communities. In this work, those working with a community might use definitional ceremonies, similar to outsider-witness practices, after a time of consultation with the community about themes. A programme is agreed that provides conditions in which devalued knowledges and skills will be 'identified, rendered more visible, richly described and honoured. Under these conditions the sophistication of these knowledges and skills become known, and the relevance of these to present circumstances is appreciated ... This opens up a range of culturally sensitive and appropriate options for community action' (White, 2003: 26).

There are many useful practical texts (Bird, 2000; Freeman *et al.*, 1997; Morgan, 1999; Morgan, 2000; White and Epston, 1990; Winslade and Monk, 1999) and lots of texts to develop the ideas and thinking behind narrative practices (Burr, 1995; White, 2004; White and Epston, 1990). Many referred to here do both. Useful websites that provide papers giving, amongst other things, more about the ideas and how they are used and invitations to training courses:

http://www.narrativepractice.co
http://www.narrativebooks.co.uk/
http://www.dulwichcentre.com.au/homepage.html

Solution-orientated working

Solution-focused or solution-orientated working focuses attention on solutions rather than the problem therefore reducing the need for professional input into problem analysis. There are many related versions of solution-focused practices, including solution-focused brief therapy, solution-orientated schools, and possibility approaches.

Constructivist assumptions

Constructivism underlies solution-focused thinking: people's problems are the result of the ways in which they construe themselves and the world. They think of themselves in terms of the problem and depict the problem as always happening. Exceptions – times when the problem is absent or less in evidence – are dismissed. Exceptions are open to view but are not seen by the client as 'the differences that makes the difference' (de Shazer, 1991: 58). For the client the problem is seen as primary and the exceptions, if they are seen at all, as secondary. For therapists it is the other way around – the exceptions are seen as primary. The aim of therapy is for the client to have this perspective too, which leads to the development of a soluation (de Shazer, 1991).

Assumptions

The conversational strategies supported by solution-focused approaches are rich ways for exploring the kinds of solutions a child or (adult or family) wants for his or her (or their) own life or lives. Solutions can be found to be already emerging in the form of exceptions. Resources and skills are made visible rather than deficits and problems. The assumptions made in this approach about children and families and about professional role align themselves very closely to many in the PPC Model presented in Chapter 6. The techniques and ideas are fully centred on the development of a collaborative relationship between practitioners and those with whom they work.

Solution-focused thinking makes certain assumptions about people and their problems, and about the role of those who assist people with their problems. Problems are things people want to do without – they are not looked at in terms of a symptom of something else or underlying causes. People are believed to have the skills, resources and qualities they will need to resolve their difficulties, and these strengths are key to the basis for change. Assumptions underlying the role of therapist and client vary a little depending upon the writer, but include: therapy as a collaborative process, the therapist as having expertise; an orientation towards the present and optimism about the future; searching for and noticing client competencies, strengths and resources; and an avoidance of a search for causes, pathology or labels.

Tools and practices

Practitioners adopt a stance of curiosity about beliefs, actions, views and behaviour. A number of ways of talking are suggested and developed – either one-to-one or in meetings – in order to establish belief in people's resources and capacity for change, and to focus on what the child, family or community feel is important. There are a range of future-orientated questions that enable some creative conversations about people's hopes for a future without the problem and help to clarify goals. Future orientated conversations can enable more understanding about what is already happening – about exceptions to the problem. The use of a scale from 0 to 10 can enable a dialogue about where the person would like to be, and how far they have already come. A miracle question may be used which asks a client to share a vision of what their life would look like, what they would experience, if the problem was absent. This helps to develop detail about where a person would like to be, and there follows a conversation about what might be the first step towards this, or (again) what is already happening. There is an assumption that if something works, do more of it – but if it doesn't, stop. This comes from the observation that many attempts as solving problems only serve to maintain them.

> The task of the worker is to highlight in conversation what appear to be solution thoughts and behaviours and thus guide the conversation towards new ways of thinking and doing that may make a difference.
>
> (Amjal and Rees, 2001: 12)

Well documented key features of a solution-focused therapy session include:

- setting goal(s);
- the use of the miracle question;
- use of scaling questions;
- a search for exceptions;
- a consultation break;
- feedback – on the strengths of the client (compliments) and the setting of a task.

A solution-focused school

Solution-focused schools might use ideas and practice from solution-focused thinking within aspects of the whole school. Solution-orientated schools may have a teacher who acts as a solution-focused co-ordinator. This person acts as a supervisor to other teachers in dealing with any problem that arises. Problems that persist trigger solution-focused meetings involving parents. Solution-orientated thinking is also brought into the management and development of schools.

A solution-focused meeting

Michael Harker compares problem-solving approaches to meetings with a solutions approach to meetings (Harker, 2001). A problem-solving framework involves most time in the meeting being spent on problem talk, and includes conversation about, for example, the case history, reports on past and current professional involvement and planning what to do next. Alternatively, a solution-building meeting involves discussions about what has worked in the past and what people are doing to cope. It involves identifying and describing goals, and exceptions. Possible activities might include:

- listening to descriptions of the problem, in order to uncover exceptions and competencies;
- discussions about what people are doing to cope with the situation;
- descriptions of exceptions;
- discussions to make exceptions meaningful;
- discussions about what has worked in the past;
- scaling questions;
- identifying and describing goals;
- establishing and agreeing tasks.

(Harker, 2001: 34)

Other applications

Many workers from a range of professional backgrounds are using solution-focused ideas and techniques in many different and very creative ways. This way of working is being applied to every kind of problem, and to conversations with individuals, groups and whole schools. A selection of the particular applications that can assist in the development of inclusive education are as follows (Amjal and Rees, 2001; Rhodes and Ajmal, 1995):

- solution-focused anti-bullying approaches;
- training children in solution-focused approaches to use in peer support schemes in schools;
- using solution focused thinking in consultation conversations between teachers and educational psychologists;
- solution-focused group-work with children experiencing difficulties in behaviour;
- solution-focused family work;
- using solution-focused ideas with children experiencing difficulties with reading;
- a solution-focused way of thinking about teaching and learning;
- applying a solutions approach to multidisciplinary child protection processes;
- applying the ideas of solution-focused thinking to change in organisations via 'appreciative inquiry'.

There are many other practical texts to assist in the development of this kind of work (de Shazer, 1985; de Shazer, 1991; Durrant, 1995). Useful websites for solution-focused and solution-orientated ways of working, from which a large number of references can be found as well as invitations to training courses, are:

http://www.sycol.co.uk/default.htm
www.brief-therapy.org

This chapter moves now from general practices (narrative and solution) to four case studies that exemplify the PPC Model of collaborative practice, or have potential to model such practice.

Case study 1

Transforming learning in schools: democratic RE

The changes in classroom ethos and the greater engagement with ideas through a process of collaborative enquiry that has been in evidence through the use of some thinking skills approaches can be seen as inclusive education in action. A good example of this is the use of 'Philosophy for Children' via a community of enquiry in RE teaching. For a number of years, lecturers and research associates from the Research Centre for Teaching and Learning at Newcastle University have developed research partnerships with schools and Local Education Authorities in the north-east of England and nationally that aim to develop creative approaches to teaching and learning.

In using 'Philosophy for Children' in RE, a story or piece of narrative from the writings of, for example, Christianity, Judaism, Sufi stories or the Islamic tradition provides the starting point for the following process:

- The whole class listens to a short story or extract.
- Pupils think of questions they would like to ask.
- Pupils discuss questions in pairs or groups and choose one question for the whole class to discuss.
- Teacher scribes the questions for whole-class discussion on a whiteboard or flip chart.
- Pupils decide the order in which to discuss the questions.
- The discussion begins with the pupils whose question has been chosen giving their thoughts.
- Pupils then join in by either agreeing or disagreeing with previous contributions and they must give a reason, for example, 'I agree/disagree with . . . because . . .'.
- The class work their way through as many questions as they can in the time with a view to arriving as some consensus/conclusions from the discussion.

(Baumfield, 2003: 181)

Evaluations have revealed changes that suggest a move towards a transformative approach to teaching and learning (Baumfield, 2002; Davies, 1995; Williams, 1993). Using thinking skills strategies in the classroom enables significant shifts to occur in the patterns of classroom interaction in a relatively short time whilst engaging pupils so classroom management is less of an issue. The focus for teachers and learners shifts from narrowly perceived outcomes, i.e. factual recall, to a deeper engagement with the processes of learning. Pupils develop their ability to raise questions for themselves, to interrogate texts more meaningfully, and to look at issues in more depth and with more understanding. A study of impact found pupils had greater intellectual confidence – not only about their own performance at school but also about their ability to contribute to society. They were more able to examine assumptions, provide reasons for their views, and listen to the views of others. The traditional 'IRE' pattern of interaction (teacher Initiation usually through a closed question, pupil Response, teacher Evaluation) was disrupted, children were found to take a more active role, and pupil–pupil interactions were altered. Positive effects were reported on children who were normally shy and withdrawn. Teachers report that it is often those pupils who do not normally participate who excel in these lessons. An ethos of respect was found to have developed. There were also fewer demands on the teacher to spoonfeed pupils with set answers and more opportunity to extend and develop pupils' thinking.

The resistance of classroom practice to change, noted in research, has been overcome by the use of a collaborative process of classroom research which also necessitated a network of support involving researchers and teachers. Also key to success is thought to be:

- an explicit rationale with a strong theoretical basis;
- well-designed contextualised teaching materials;
- an explicit pedagogy; and
- good teacher support.

This case involves a critical approach to the prevalent transmission understandings of learning and teaching. The university researchers took a de-centred role in working with the teachers to honour teachers' values, their hopes for their own teaching, and the rich stories of their knowledges of teaching. The outcome was learning that more richly described identities of both teachers and pupils.

Case study 2

Involving children and young people in decision-making and in the development of services: 'Investing in Children'

Investing in Children was created in County Durham in the mid 1990s, funded jointly by the health, social services and education departments in the county, and it now has a large number of partner organisations. Its aim is to consult with children, young people and their families about decisions affecting their lives and the development of services. It has developed an innovative model of working with young people that strives to be inclusive. The way it works has enabled it to learn from mistakes and develop ways to structure the different involvement of adults and young people so that the voices of young people can be heard, and young people can develop skills, understanding and confidence. The organisation supports children and young people to contribute to debates and campaigns for change in issues they have identified as important or to respond to the requests from external organisations to consult young people on particular matters. IiC also has a membership scheme to try to develop change at a local level, engages in policy work to enable young people to contribute to the development of local and national policy, and is engaged by other organisations to deliver training in strategies to engage with children and young people.

It recognises that 'children and young people have a legitimate, and often revealing perspective of the world in which they live, and adults must learn to listen to them and involve them in decision-making with effects them' (Information Sheet 4, IiC, 2004). Part of the ethos is that services must include and be accessible to everyone, and that all children and young people must be treated with dignity.

Research and campaign work has been carried out in a large number of areas. Early lesson were that, when given the opportunity, the young people IiC worked with were 'willing and able to think independently and articulate an agenda of issues based upon their own experiences' (Information Sheet 5, IiC, 2004). There seemed to be common threads in the agendas of young people in different parts of the county that varied from the priorities being discussed by service providers. What seemed to be particularly important was a strategy of establishing and resourcing young people's research teams. When IiC has an area to research, a project typically starts with an 'Agenda Day'. This creates space for groups of young people (20–30) to get together to agree the agenda – what, from their perspective are the key questions. Often, several young people who have already been part of previous research projects take the role of facilitators to the whole group. Smaller groups emerge from the 'Agenda Days' focusing on particular issues. These work as research teams to explore issues, either by canvassing views of other young people, gathering information from services, or finding out how other people have approached the problem. Most research teams create some form of report, and use this to enter into dialogue with the key agencies they wish to influence.

Three of the many research projects have been as follows:

1. '730+ Bishop Auckland Diabetic Group': an IiC research team of young people with diabetes visited Sweden to look at alternative treatment models. A longer period of campaign followed on their return, assisted by a great deal of work from a consultant, and treatment options available in Durham have now been changed, consistent with the recommendations of the young people.

2. 'Fresh paint in your nostrils!' Ofsted inspection project: IiC was approached to run a project aimed at finding out from children and young people how an Ofsted inspection should hear and respond to the views of children and young people. A planning group of young people and an adult worker from IiC convened an Agenda Day attended by 26 young people in a local theatre. First

they spent time talking about their lives and the issues that are important to them, then they discussed the five questions the inspectors thought they needed answers in order to get inspections right, and then they asked questions to a member of Ofsted and someone from the National Youth Agency. There were many important views expressed, amongst these were that:

a   Inspections are false and are feared but should be more open and honest, welcomed and lead to change.
b   Inspectors should talk to all young people, not just the school council as the latter was often not representative of the views of everyone.
c   The idea of being involved in inspections was attractive as long as it led to changes in services. Young people did not know that services other than schools had inspections, but this was welcomed.

3.   'The Mask of CAMHS' The face behind the mask: IiC was commissioned by CAMHS in Teeside to look at how CAMHS could create a strategy for the participation of children and young people in its future development. IiC organised a number of Agenda Days across the Tees area. These days were facilitated by five adult and two young people facilitators, and were attended by fifteen young people. The Agenda Days included discussions on what people knew of CAMHS, what they thought of counsellors, what they thought of the name of the service, and what they had hoped to achieve by coming to the meetings. The ideas that arose from these days were about the need for a name change, confidentiality issues, the role of counsellors, and medication. Eleven young people became involved in the further research programme that resulted from the Agenda Days. This group devised a process to interview CAMHS workers, carried out the interviews, transcribed them and mapped the responses. Findings were written up as a report and presented to an invited audience of service providers (Barnett *et al.*, 2005).

IiC is an organisation that operates in ways consistent with the assumptions about people, professional practice and context identified in the PPC Model. It explicitly recognises the need to break down professional and political barriers. It has developed, and continues to develop, ways that adults, children and young people can work together to enable the voice of the child to have a real influence on the changes made to services.

Case study 3

Family Group Conferences

Family Group Conferences (FGC) structure discussions in ways that give family groups much more control over decision-making in welfare issues. Developed in New Zealand, with an origin in Maori community decision-making processes, they are used in many parts of the UK and in several other parts of the world. Common reasons for convening a FGC include problems in managing a child, questions over custody, a child protection issue or the development of different 'plans' such as a bereavement plan, a support plan for learning disability and a family support plan. There are variations in how they are organised, but they tend to have five stages:

- Stage 1: *Preparation* – a family worker consults with family members and professionals in order to agree the membership and venue of the conference. The venue is decided by the family and can be at a school, hotel, community centre, sports centre, social work offices etc.
- Stage 2: *Information sharing* – full information about the problem is shared by family members. Family members are able to question the professionals. There may be rules that bar professionals from opinion-giving about the situation or outcome.
- Stage 3: *Family conference* – the family debates the issues and produce ideas for a plan in a closed private session. The question might be, for example, was the child neglected or abused and if so, what needs to occur to ensure the child is cared for and protected from future harm.
- Stage 4: *The decision* – the family reaches a decision about their needs and a family plan required. The professionals return to the meeting and the family explains their decision. The professionals and the family discuss how the plan can be implemented, who will be involved, what resources are possible, what support is being asked from professionals and whether there are things that cannot be implemented.
- Stage 5: *The implementation* – the agreed plan is implemented.

The advantages of Family Group Conferences dovetail with much of the Practice–People–Context Model, described in detail in Chapter 6, in that they:

- empower families to take their own decisions;
- represent a repositioning of professionals with respect to clients, valuing family strengths rather than deficits. The professional is de-centred, so rather than understanding the professional as the source of knowledge about the family, the family members themselves are centred as knowledgeable;
- foster collaboration within families and between families and professionals; and
- generate unique and creative solutions.

A study funded by the Nuffield Foundation looked at eighty Family Group Conferences involving 99 children from 69 families. Nearly two-thirds of family outcomes were followed up over twelve months. Those interviewed in the research were professionals rather than family members. Findings showed the conferences were used predominantly where concerns related to neglect and less where there were concerns about physical or sexual abuse. Fifty-two per cent of the social workers involved had been surprised by the outcome:

> The ones I thought would develop a plan didn't and those that I didn't, did.

> I think the expectation of the meeting was that it was likely to be very aggressive and very violent, but in fact it wasn't at all. That was defused quite quickly and quite easily within that group setting.

> (Crow and Marsh, 1997: 13)

The Sheffield/Nuffield study found that an average of six family members attended the conferences with a wide age range, including parents, children, grandparents, aunts and uncles, cousins, siblings, step-family members and friends. Between 74 and 93 per cent of the conferences investigated made plans agreed by all parties. Comparison with plans made in other contacts (i.e. child protection conferences and review meetings) found that the families included more multi-agency work in their plans than professionals do. Social workers were generally impressed by the plans produced, incorporating ideas they thought social services would never have thought of. Family members (data from a range of other studies) (Crow and Marsh, 1997: 17) indicated satisfaction that plans were being carried out and most family participants indicated satisfaction with the process. Overall, Crow and Marsh (1997: 15) found that three-quarters of plans were being carried out successfully and were stable at a year's follow-up. Family members in another survey (Barker and Barker, 1995) reported feeling positively about the way the meeting got the family together and led to more communication. They felt more in control and appreciated the way that neutral territory and the informal atmosphere enabled people to have their say. Some members voiced concern over confidentiality in the information-sharing stage.

The main area in question in terms of putting forward FGCs as a medium for collaboration is the quality of the participation of children. From existing research, whilst children were expected to attend their conference, this seemed only to apply to young people over the age of 10 and younger children seemed not to attend. There is very little attempt in current research to document the views of children and young people about the process or outcomes of Family Group Conferences. An unpublished MSc dissertation found family workers organising conferences in one area in the North of England to have a number of reasons to be reluctant to consult with children about their views, or to invite them to meetings (Hughes, 2002). However, other studies quoted in Crow and Marsh (1997: 15) suggest that, whilst there is much room for improvement in the degree of involvement of children and young people in Family Group Conferences, more happens in this context than in other forms of family decision-making, such as review meetings, planning meetings and child protection conferences.

Family Group Conferences present a rare opportunity for a community, the wider family group, to be the agent of change. A structured process enables the practitioner to work in a de-centred role and provide spaces for different knowledges, of various family members, and of the professionals to be heard and to influence different care decisions.

Case study 4

Extended schools

Extended schools deliberately focus attention beyond the core concern of teaching and learning in the classroom.

> An extended school maximises the curricular learning of its pupils by promoting their overall development and by ensuring that the family and community contexts within which they live are as supportive of learning as possible.
>
> (Cummings *et al.*, 2004)

The typical range of activities that might comprise an extended school includes:

- wraparound childcare on school site;
- varied out of school hours activities for school-aged children, parenting support;
- easy referral to a wide range of specialist support services (many delivered on school site);
- community access to ICT, arts and sports facilities and to adult learning.

(HMSO, 2003)

Over the last few years there has been funding in England and Scotland for some extended schools in each local authority (Sammons *et al.*, 2003; Cummings *et al.*, 2005). The funding of pilot schools has led to the development of the policy nationally (Cummings *et al.*, 2004).

Extended schools represent one of the answers to the acknowledgement that social inclusion problems in areas of economic disadvantage can only be tackled through collaboration between the different agencies, as discussed at length in Chapter 5. An example of the kind of strategic approach that can be taken is shown in Exhibit 2.2 from the national evaluation of extended schools in England (Cummings *et al.*, 2005). Interviews carried out with head teachers and extended school co-ordinators in schools that had received government funding (Dyson *et al.*, 2002; Cummings *et al.*, 2004; Cummings *et al.*, 2005) found inclusion (and various understanding of what inclusion is about) an explicit aim of a minority of extended schools visited, but implicit in the reported aims and rationales of all. Analysis of the kinds of activities, provisions and partnerships being developed in the extended schools researched in the three projects evidenced many examples that could be said to lie within an inclusion agenda.

Exhibit 2.2: a strategic approach

LA7 offers an example of a strategic approach that extends well beyond the school. Two secondary schools are developing as FSESs (full service extended schools), and are working closely with the primaries in each cluster. The schools, which are located in adjacent inner-city areas, serve six of the ten most deprived wards in the borough. The head teachers and assistant head

teachers in both schools work closely to plan FSES developments, offer mutual support and share good practice. Both FSESs
work in partnership with the LEA and their feeder primaries.

The FSES model 'acts as a concept and framework through
which services and programmes are delivered'.

The FSES model was developed by the local community,
voluntary workers, children and young people and officers in
partnership. A multi-agency training event for professionals
supported by the LA, the PCT and the workforce development
confederation was integral to the development of the model
although much groundwork had been done and much had
been achieved in the ten years preceding. The FSES model forms
'an essential element of [the Local Authority's] strategy for
reducing inequality, narrowing attainment gaps and tackling
underachievement'.

It is managed in each school by the assistant head teacher for
inclusion with the support of other members of the senior leadership team, and in the local authority, it is managed by a senior
officer with the support of colleagues. In the LA, the FSES model
sits within the structure of the Local Strategic Partnership (LSP)
and the Children, Young Persons and Families Delivery Board
and associated local implementation team. FSES is embedded
within a range of initiatives including BIP, EiC, specialist colleges
and local regeneration initiatives. Network co-ordination meetings take place on a regular basis to facilitate multi-agency
planning and delivery.

(Cummings *et al.*, 2005: 16)

The provision of schools sampled at the end of the first year of the
national roll-out in England was vast and varied (Cummings *et al.*,
2005). Most schools offered out of hours provision for pupils which
might involve breakfast clubs, study support, sports, arts and ICT-
based extra-curricular activities, holiday schemes and so on. Many
delivered some childcare from the school. Adult education and family
learning was also offered in most schools and there was invariably a
community use component to their work. Extended schools tended to
offer this variety of provision and some offered other innovative programmes such as intergenerational programmes or crime prevention
strands. Some schools offered all or some of the following; healthcare
(this might be health clinics comprising of sexual health services, falls

clinic, men's health provision, pre- and antenatal support, smoking cessation, nutritional advice, speech and language and mental health provision etc.), social care (this might involve having a resident social worker on site), crime initiatives (this might involve having drop-in sessions with the police, junior neighbourhood watch, solving problem programmes), and family support (this might involve the establishment of family support teams, the appointment of home–school liaison officers, offering parenting programmes etc.).

There is much anecdotal evidence from pupils, parents and community members of increased involvement in learning as a result of the activities offered in extended schools. Extended schools have already shown great potential for creative projects that consume and generate the energy of all involved. Everything from a 7-day radio station broadcast from school, a garden development in the school playground involving artists, children, teachers and parents, and a history project involving joint visits between a group of mature community members and school pupils.

Extended schools offer a great deal of potential for collaboration between the practitioners of different agencies, children and young people, and parents and community members (see Exhibit 2.3). Some of it appears, from research, to be in the process of being realised. Many schools are operating a co-location model which brings together professionals from statutory, voluntary and community organisations together on the school site. There are some pupil and community involvement elements. This might involve pupils and community members sitting on the FSES steering group and being involved in decision-making, school councils, pupil leadership schemes, community service volunteering, pupils consulting community members or working with them on particular projects. Many of the projects developed by extended schools seem to have the effect of putting children and parents in the position that the rich stories of their lives are more available to the school than any thin problem-saturated story. This is the case in, for example, a family learning project in which children and parents learn side-by-side say in a collaboration with artists. Or a collaboration between teachers, children, families, artist and landscape gardeners to visit the newly opened modern art gallery and redesign the school playground. Or in the development by young people and the community of a community cinema. Or the week-long 24-hour broadcast of a radio station from the school, managed only by pupils.

However, there is evidence that the rationales articulated by the schools about what it means to them to be 'extended' and how they

Exhibit 2.3: inter-agency working in extended schools

The FSES in LA10 is an example of a full service extended approach as integral to the work of the school, rather than as a bolt-on to existing provision. It also demonstrates how an FSES can facilitate links with different agencies. It is a large multi-ethnic community secondary school applying for Arts and Media Specialist status and with plans for PFI rebuild. A City Learning Centre is located on site as is a purpose-built expressive arts building for music, drama and art. The school currently draws many of its population from a neighbourhood renewal area, characterised by a high level of deprivation and with a largely transient school population including refugees and asylum seekers. However, the school would like its intake to reflect the diversity of its whole catchment area, which also includes a significant middle-class population. To create a more mixed and stable intake, the school is pursuing initiatives – such as the development of a Parent Teacher Association – to encourage the mixed local community across the threshold. Community use of the school attracts a wider population including Japanese and Armenian families. Low aspirations, often reported as a problem by FSESs, are not seen as such here, since the migrant communities in particular have high expectations for their children. Trying to meet these expectations simply from within its own resources, however, seems to the school to be impracticable, given the range of needs which it has to meet. In this situation, FSES status offers an alternative means of addressing children's difficulties: 'A lot of the work we do, just because of the nature of the students, if it's not community based then we don't get as a far as we should' (Head teacher)

   In view of its challenging situation, the school has a history of offering extended provision. Newcomers to the school, regardless of their ethnic origin, tend to bring issues that need addressing as swiftly as possible. The recently appointed FSES co-ordinator has done much to introduce different community organisations to one another and this has improved the perception of the school by local families. Out of school activities, especially around the arts, encourage greater community involvement. Community links are maintained with support from the Youth Service which can target families at an early stage. Within school, early intervention strategies include the addition of learning mentors, the learning support unit, counselling and outreach support undertaken through the Child and Adolescent Mental Health Service (CAMHS). Additional specialist help, for instance from the Somalian Liaison Group, is essential. Wider links have been established by means of the school's designation as a BIP school which has established liaison with CAMHS, through CYPSP, the children's trust and the Vulnerable Children's Service. Outcomes intended by the school include a change in local people's perceptions of the school (with the help of PFI) and greater representation of the middle-class community; inclusion (understood as a school that is valued by the whole community); a stable school with improved social and emotional health; community cohesion; and the raised achievement of young people.

(Cummings *et al.*, 2005: 19)

conceptualise their communities are principally based on the perspectives of the professionals involved. Pupils, parents and communities seem to have had little role in the direction of the extended school. Interestingly, in most cases pupils are approached positively by teaching staff, with high expectations, but the communities in which they live are considered in very broadly deficit terms.

It remains to be seen in the coming years, as extended schools develop further, whether they are able to readjust power relationships to enable greater moves towards collaborative working.

Appendix
What kind of services do children and young people want?

Chapter 7 related how children and young people have often been kept in the dark about services they use and how some attempts to hear their views can leave them more disadvantaged if they do not understand the role of the professional or the context of the decision-making that is happening. Evidence has also been presented about the relative lack of participatory practice that is going on – with some clear examples of good practice and relationships with professionals that are very much appreciated by young people. From this varied research evidence, and also from research by young people and others into what young people want in services, it is possible to put together a list of areas that are *it seems, to the author*, likely to be more helpful to children and young people. These are just a starting point. They are not a guide to service providers to follow. They are the first steps towards working with young people to research your service to find out what they think and how you should deliver your service.

Clear information about who they are dealing with and a choice about who to see: 'Can you change that name?'

Children and young people want services that easily and clearly communicate to them want they are about, so that they can know how – and whether – to use them. Research suggests young people may have the following preferences:

- to be given a choice about whether to use a service;
- a choice about who to see;
- services that are easy to use – i.e. to approach services directly without the need for 'referral' (Lingard, 2002), email doctors'

surgeries or contraception mailing service, access to leisure services (Troman and Sangster, 2003);

- young people said they wanted brief information, clearly presented, and not necessarily translated into Bangla and Urdu as most young people, of those part of this sample. read only English (Lingard, 2002).

Children and young people have views on the people they see when they have problems:

- in one study children said there were no professionals they could trust (Roose and John, 2003), but they might be able to talk to a nurse, friend or relative;
- there was a general dissatisfaction with the service provided by GPs, and the comments of these young people suggested that their needs would best be met by a one-stop shop for health advice, counselling and social services (DfES, 2003: 51 quoting Thorpe, 2003);
- children said it would not be culturally acceptable for some children to talk outside the family, confidentiality is mistrusted;
- children and young people can talk of what it is about certain workers that they like and in others that they don't (Tolley *et al.*, 1998);
- teachers, other professionals and parents may not be as favoured as peers as people to talk to about problems (Tolley *et al.*, 1998; Armstrong *et al.*, 2000; Roose and John, 2003): 'Teachers were not thought to be a safe choice for help by some participants owing to reasons of confidentiality' (Roose and John, 2003: 547);
- social workers should care more about education 'they just see you more like an animal that's got to be fed, watered, clothed and sheltered somewhere. Once they get that sorted its just lets pass the buck to someone else' (16-year-old in foster care) (Harker *et al.*, 2003: 95), but also teachers should know more about the pressures of being in care.

Children and young people had views about the names of certain professionals, their organisations and the labels they used and wanted words like 'educational psychologist', 'CAMHS' and 'mental health' to be changed.

What happens during a consultation should have certain qualities

Young people have views about what happens to them when they see professionals, and would like to be informed to the extent that they can have an opinion about what happens to them, be it treatment, assessment, mentoring or counselling. Children's views about the content of what happens may vary from child to child and depending upon the situation and the kind of professional. The following are likely to be key requirements:

- to be given information about their rights (Harker *et al.*, 2003);
- they want to understand what is going on (Aubrey and Dahl, 2006);
- they may also want to have a say in what happens – to be seriously consulted regarding decisions affecting their lives (Harker *et al.*, 2003);
- to be prepared for meetings (Aubrey and Dahl, 2006);
- they also want the contact to be worthwhile. For example, the young people attending a youth club in South Yorkshire said that they wanted to see educational psychologists who wouldn't just provide information, but would spend time getting actively involved, talking to them to understand what is happening (Lingard, 2002);
- staff should have personal experience, be welcoming, have professional expertise, be interesting and confidential; and
- young people have views on the environment in which they see people. Ideas included not having to travel but out of school as they wouldn't want everyone to know they were going for help: 'others might believe it was an issue to do with them and be upset' (Roose and John, 2003: 548). Some young people wanted services that were based in attractive welcoming places where they could have fun and not just focus on their difficulties (DfES, 2003: 51 quoting Thorpe, 2003).

Quotes from some young people:

- think about your accent and the way you speak;
- don't talk too much and think about your body language;
- don't use big, complicated or confusing words, or 'old' or posh language;
- try to be friendly, relax and smile more, and make the young people feel welcome;

- don't look down on us or have a negative attitude;
- put yourself in the young person's shoes, get down to their level, and show respect;
- always be on time – waiting is boring.

(Lingard, 2002)

Confidentiality and control over use of information about them

There is a lot of discussion about how to create a record system open to all professionals that enable children not to become lost in a system and enable them to be given services they need. However, this debate very often omits the consideration of the children and young people themselves, that they might not want information about their difficulties to be known to others. We do not have much information about their views in this area. We do know that some children and young people wanted services that had clear policies on confidentiality (Thorpe, 2003). However, Lingard found that young people wanted honest and informative individual reports, but written for themselves rather than for others (Lingard, 2002). Young people researching CAMHS as part of Investing in Children found that confidentiality and ownership were important to young people. For example, some of the young people looking at the CAMHS service felt strongly that their parents should not be included in their counselling sessions (Gimrax and Bell, 2004). In a study of fifteen looked-after children aged 10 to 15, several felt let down when what they had said to a social worker was written in the file (Munro, 2001). Others praised counsellors for offering a confidential relationship.

Inclusivity

There is a general theme in research of young people wanting the needs of particular young people to be met, but to be met in a way that does not single them out or cause stigma or embarrassment. Young people tend not to want to be treated as different to other young people – and they wanted all young people to have access to help (DfES, 2003; Thorpe, 2003). For example, Investing in Children looked at the use of a concessions card in Durham for use in sports and leisure services. Young people expressed concern, since, when this card was used it drew attention to the young person's status as looked after (Cairns and Brannon, 2005: 82). Similarly, the Drive project, provision of driving lessons for looked-after young people, involved aspects that amounted to a disincentive to attend. This included the requirement to attend a day-long course on road safety with the police before the lessons could be taken up, the requirement to use a national provider rather than local providers, and the requirement on instructors to write reports on the progress of their students (Cairns and Brannon, 2005). Following consultation, the road safety session has been dropped, local providers can be used and reports are no longer required. Children and young people are also very tolerant of special assistance being given to those who need it.

Bibliography

Ainscow, M. (1999) *Understanding the Development of Inclusive Schools* (London, Falmer).

Ainscow, M., Farrell, P., Tweddle, D. and Malki, G. (1999) *Effective Practice in Inclusion, and in Special and Mainstream Schools Working Together* (Manchester, Centre for Educational Needs, University of Manchester with Oldham MBC).

Ainscow, M., Howes, A., Farrell, P. and Frankham, J. (2003) Making sense of the development of inclusive practices, *European Journal of Special Educational Needs*, 18(2), pp. 227–242.

Alderson, P. (2000) Children's rights and school councils, *Children and Society*, 14(2), pp. 21–34.

Aldridge, J. (2003) Listening at doors. Young people's perspectives of the treatment they received from adult professionals after sexual abuse was discovered (B.Sc. undergraduate unpublished report, Newcastle University).

Aldridge, J. and Becker, S. (1994) *My Child, My Carer – the Parents' Perspective* (Loughborough, Loughborough University).

Allen, J. (1999) *Actively Seeking Inclusion. Pupils with Special Needs in Mainstream Schools* (London, Falmer Press).

Amjal, Y. and Rees, I. (eds) (2001) *Solutions in Schools* (London, Brief Therapy Press).

Armstrong, C., Hill, M. and Secker, J. (2000) Young people's perceptions of mental health, *Children and Society*, 14, pp. 60–72.

Armstrong, D. (1995) *Power and Partnership in Education* (London, Routledge).

Armstrong, D., Galloway, D. and Tomlinson, S. (1993) The assessment of special educational needs and the proletarianisation of professionals, *British Journal of Sociology*, 14(4), pp. 399–408.

Armstrong, D., Dolinski, R. and Wrapson, C. (1999) What about Chantel? From inside out: an insider's experience of exclusion, *International Journal of Inclusive Education*, 3(1), pp. 27–36.

Arora, T. and Mackay, L. (2004) Talking and listening to children diagnosed with ADHD and taking psychostimulants, in: T. Billington and

M. Pomerantz (eds) *Children at the Margins. Supporting Children. Supporting Schools* (Stoke-on-Trent, Trentham).

Atkinson, M., Wilkin, A., Stott, A. and Kinder, K. (2001) *Multi-Agency Working: An Audit of Activity. LGA Research Report 17* (Slough, NFER).

Aubrey, C. and Dahl, S. (2006) Children's voices: the views of vulnerable children on their service providers and the relevance of services they receive, *British Journal of Social Work*, 36, pp. 21–39.

Bagley, C., Woods, P.A. and Woods, G. (2001) Implementation of school choice policy: interpretation and response by parents of students with special educational needs, *British Educational Research Journal*, 27(3), pp. 287–311.

Bailey, G. (1993) You won't get me involved – I'm a plumber, in: R. Merttens, D. Mayers, A. Brown and J. Vass (eds) *Ruling the Margins: Problematising Parental Involvement* (London, IMPACT Project, University of North London).

Barker, J., Smith, F., Morrow, V., Weller, S., Hey, V. and Harwin, J. (2003) *The Impact of Out of School Care: A Qualitative Study Examining the Views of Children, Families and Playworkers* (Brunel University).

Barker, S.O. and Barker, R. (1995) *A Study of the Experiences and Perceptions of 'Family' and 'Staff' Perceptions in Family Group Conferences.* (Gwynnedd Porthaethwy, MEDRA Research Group).

Barnett, R., Grego, K., Youll, K., Corcoran, A., Shuttleworth, S., Brown, L., McCartney, R., Campbell, L., Morris, M., Brown, K., Barnett, N., Stampet, S., Hussain, I. and Bell, P. (2005) *The Masks of CAMHS. The Face Behind the Mask* (Durham, Investing in Children and Tees and North East Yorkshire NHS Trust).

Barton, L. and Moody, S. (1981) The value of parents to the ESN(S) school: an examination, in: L. Barton and S. Tomlinson (eds) *Special Education: Policy, Practices and Social Issues* (London, Harper and Row).

Bastiani, J. (ed.) (1987) *Parents and Teachers 1: Perspectives on Home–School Relations* (Windsor, NFER-Nelson).

Baumfield, V. (ed.) (2002) *Thinking Through RE* (Cambridge, Chris Kington Publishing).

Baumfield, V. (2003) Democratic RE: preparing young people for citizenship, *British Journal of Religious Education*, 25(3), pp. 173–184.

Beveridge, S. (2005) *Children, Families and Schools. Developing Partnerships for Inclusive Education* (Abingdon, RoutledgeFalmer).

Billington, T. (2000) *Separating, Losing and Excluding Children. Narratives of Difference* (London, Falmer).

Billington, T. and Pomerantz, M. (eds) (2004) *Children at the Margins. Supporting Children, Supporting Schools* (Stoke-on-Trent, Trentham Books).

Billington, T., McNally, B. and NcNally, C. (2000) Autism: working with parents, and discources in experience, expertise and learning, *Educational Psychology in Practice*, 16(1), pp. 59–68.

Bird, J. (2000) *The Heart's Narrative* (Auckland, Edge Press).

Black, P. and Williams, D. (1998) *Inside the Black Box: Raising Standards through Classroom Assessment* (London, King College London School of Education).

Blatchford, P. (1996a) Pupils' views of school work and school from 7 to 16 years, *Research Papers in Education*, 11(3), pp. 263–288.

Blatchford, P. (1996b) Taking pupils seriously. Recent research and initiatives on breaktime in school, *Education 3 to 13*, October, pp. 60–65.

Boag-Munroe, G. (2004) Wrestling with words and meanings: finding a tool for analysing language in activity theory, *Education Review*, 56(2), pp. 165–182.

Booth, T. (2003) Viewing inclusion from a distance: gaining perspective from comparative study, in: M. Nind, J. Rix, K. Sheehy and K. Simmons (eds) *Inclusive Education: Diverse Perspectives* (London, David Fulton).

Border, R. and Merttens, R. (1993) Parental partnership: comfort or conflict?, in: R. Merttens and J. Vass (eds) *Partnerships in Maths: Parents and Schools* (London, Falmer Press).

Bourdieu, P. (1977) *Outline of a Theory of Practice* (New York, Cambridge University Press).

Bourdieu, P. (1986) The forms of capital, in: J. Richardson (ed.) *Handbook of Theory and Research for the Sociology of Education* (New York, Greenwood).

Brown, C. (1994) Parents and professionals: future directions, in: K. Ballard (ed.) *Disability, Family, Whanau and Society* (Palmerston North, Dunmore Press).

Brown, K. and White, K. (2006) *Exploring the Evidence Base for Integrated Children's Services* (Edinburgh, Scottish Executive Education Department).

Bullock, A. (1975) *A Language for Life. Report of the Committee of Enquiry* (London, HMSO).

Burke, C. and Grosvenor, I. (2003) *The School I'd Like. Children and Young People's Reflections on an Education for the 21st Century* (London, RoutledgeFalmer).

Burr, V. (1995) *An Introduction to Social Construction* (London, Routledge).

Burr, V. (2002) *The Person in Social Psychology* (Hove, Psychology Press).

Caine, M. (2001) Pupils' involvement in meetings: a study to ascertain current and best practice for children deemed to have special educational needs (M.Sc. in educational psychology, dissertation, Newcastle University).

Cairns, L. (2001) Investing in children: learning how to promote the rights of all children, *Children and Society*, 15.

Cairns, L. and Brannon, M. (2005) Promoting the human rights of children and young people, *Children and Society*, 29(1), pp. 78–87.

Cameron, R.J. (1986) *Portage: Pre-schoolers, Parents and Professionals* (Windsor, NFER-Nelson).

Capper, C., Hanson, S. and Huilman, R.R. (1993) Community-based interagency collaboration: a poststructural interpretation of critical practices, *Journal of Educational Policy*, 9(4), pp. 335–351.

Carbanaro, W.J. (1998) A little help from my friends' parents: intergenerational closure and educational outcomes, *Sociology of Education*, 71, pp. 295–313.

Cassavella, A., Grove, P., Hobbs, C., Lingard, C., Jones, V., Twisleton, M. and Vickers, M. (2002) *Having a Say, Making a Change*, CD Rom Resource (Tamworth, Nasen).

Chambers, D. (2001) *Representing the Family* (London, Sage).

Chandler, L.J. (1986) Implementation of the 1981 Education Act. Parents' Perceptions of the Statementing Procedure (M.Sc. in educational psychology, dissertation, Manchester University).

CISE (2003a) *The Inclusion Charter* (http:/inclusion.uwe.ac.uk/csie/charter.htm).

Clare, L. and Cox, S. (2003) Improving service approaches and outcomes for people with complex needs through consultation and involvement, *Disability and Society*, 18(7), pp. 935–953.

Clark, A. and Moss, P. (2001) *Listening to Young Children. The Mosaic Approach* (London, National Children's Bureau and Joseph Rowntree Foundation).

Clark, A., McQuail, S. and Moss, P. (2003) *Exploring the Field of Listening to and Consulting with Young Children*, Research Report RR445 (London, DfES).

Clark, J., Dyson, A., Meagher, N., Robson, E. and Wootten, M. (eds) (2001) *Young People as Researchers. Possibilities, Problems and Politics* (Brighton, Youth Work Press).

Clarke, D. (1982) *Mentally Handicapped People* (London, Bailliere Tindall).

Clarke, F. (2006) To what extent do educational psychologists consult with children in everyday practice? (Newcastle University, unpublished undergraduate project).

Cole, M. (1996) *Cultural Psychology. A Once and Future Discipline* (London, The Belknap Press of Harvard University Press).

Coleman, J.S. (1990) *The Foundations of Social Theory* (Cambridge, MA, Cambridge University Press).

Coll, C.G., Surrey, J.L. and Weingarten, K. (eds) (1998) *Mothering Against the Odds. Diverse Voices of Contemporary Mothers* (New York, Guilford Press).

Connor, M. (2000) Asperger syndrome (autistic spectrum disorder) and the self-reports of comprehensive school students, *Educational Psychology in Practice*, 16(3), pp. 285–296.

Cook, G., Gerrish, K. and Clarke, C. (2001) Decision-making in teams: issues arising from two UK evaluations, *Journal of Interprofessional Care*, 15(2), pp. 141–151.

Cooper, P. (1993) Learning from pupils' perspectives, *British Journal of Special Education*, 20(4), pp. 129–133.

Cooper, P. and McIntyre, D. (1995) *Effective Teaching and Learning. Teachers' and Students' Perspectives* (Buckingham, Open University Press).

Corker, M. and Davis, J. (2002) Portrait of Callum. The disabling of a child-hood?, in: R. Edwards (ed.) *Children, Home and School. Regulation, Autonomy or Regulation?* (London, RoutledgeFalmer).

Cowie, H. and Wallace, P. (2000) *Peer Support in Action. From Bystanding to Standing By* (London, Sage).

Cross, J. (1989) Recording: parents, professionals and their perceptions of partnership, *Scottish Educational Review*, 21(2), pp. 106–116.

Crow, G. and Marsh, P. (1997) *Family Group Conferences, Partnerships and Child Welfare* (Sheffield, Sheffield University Press).

Crozier, G. (1996) Black parents and school relationships: a case study, *Educational Review*, 48(3), pp. 253–267.

Crozier, G. (2000) *Parents and Schools. Partners or Protagonists?* (Stoke-on-Trent, Trentham).

Crozier, G. (2005) 'There's a war against our children': black edcuational underachievement revisited, *British Journal of Sociology of Education*, 26(5), pp. 585–598.

Crozier, G. and Davies, J. (2007) Hard to reach parents or hard to reach schools? A discussion of home-school relations, with particular reference to Bangladeshi and Pakistani parents, *British Educational Research Journal*, in press.

Cummings, C., Dyson, A. and Todd, L. (2004) *Evaluation of the Extended Schools Pathfinder. Research Report 530* (London, DfES).

Cummings, C., Dyson, A., Papps, I., Pearson, D., Raffo, C. and Todd, L. (2005) *Evaluation of the Full Service Extended Schools Project: End of First Year Report* (London, DfES).

Cummings, C., Dyson, A. and Todd, L. (2007, in press) Towards extended schools? How education and other professionals understand community-orientated schooling, *Children and Society*.

Cunningham, C. and Davis, H. (1985) *Working with Parents. Frameworks for Collaboration* (Buckingham, Open University Press).

Cunningham, C. and Sloper, P. (1978) *Helping Your Handicapped Baby* (London, Souvenir Press).

Cutler, D. and Taylor, A. (2003) *Expanding and Sustaining Involvement. A Snapshot of Participation Infrastructure for Young People Living in England (Spring 2003)*, commissioned by the Children and Young People's Unit (London, DfES and Carnegie Young People Initiative).

Dale, N. (1995) *Working with Families of Children with Special Needs* (London, Routledge).

Daly, B., Addington, J., Kerfoot, S. and Sigston, A. (1985) *Portage: The Importance of Parents* (Windsor, NFER-Nelson).

Daniels, H. (1998) Researching issues of gender in special needs education, in: P. Clough and L. Barton (eds) *Articulating with Difficulty. Researching Voices in Inclusive Education* (London, Paul Chapman Publishing).

Daniels, H. (2001) *Vygotsky and Pedagogy* (London, RoutledgeFalmer).

Daniels, H. (2004) Activity theory, discourse and Bernstein, *Education Review*, 56(2), pp. 121–132.

David, M. (1993) *Parents, Gender and Education Reform* (Cambridge, Polity Press).

Davie, R. and Galloway, D. (1995) *Listening to Children* (London, David Fulton).

Davies, S. (1995) *Improving Reading Standards in Primary Schools Project* (Carmarthen, Dyfed County Council).

Davis, J., Watson, N., Corker, M. and Shakespeare, T. (2003) Reconstructing disability, childhood and social policy in the UK, in: C. Hallett and A. Prout (eds) *Hearing the Voices of Children. Social Policy for a New Century* (London, RoutledgeFalmer).

de Shazer, S. (1985) *Keys to Solutions in Brief Therapy* (New York, Norton).

de Shazer, S. (1991) *Putting Difference to Work* (New York, Norton).

DES (1955) *Report of the Committee of Maladjusted Children* (London, HMSO).

DES (1967) *Children and their Primary Schools. A Report of the Central Advisory Council for Education (England)* (London, HMSO).

DES (1978) *Special Educational Needs (The Warnock Report)* (London, HMSO).

Dessent, T. (1996) Meeting special educational needs – options for partnership between health, social and education services, in: S.P.O.S. Group (ed.) *Options for Partnership Between Health, Education and Social Services* (Tamworth, Nasen).

DFE (1994) *Code of Practice on the Identification and Assessment of Special Educational Needs* (London, DFE).

DfEE (1993) *GEST 1994–1995. Circular 10/93* (London, DFEE).

DfES (2001a) *SEN Toolkit. Section 4. Enabling Pupil Participation* (London, DfES).

DfES (2001b) *Special Educational Needs Code of Practice* (London, DfES).

DfES (2002) *14–19 Green Paper. 14–19 Extending Opportunities, Raising Standards* (London, DfES).

DfES (2003) *The Children Act. Report 2002* (London, DfES).

DfES (2004a) *Department for Education and Skills: Five Year Strategy for Children and Learners. Putting people at the heart of public services* (London, DfES).

DfES (2004b) *Every Child Matters . . . and Every Young Person. What you said and what we're going to do* (London, DfES).

DfES (2004c) *Every Child Matters: Next Steps* (London, DfES).

DfES (2005a) *Ethnicity and Education: The Evidence on Minority Ethnic Pupils*, Research Topic Paper: RTP01–05 (London, DfES).

DfES (2005b) *Higher Standards, Better Schools For All. More Choice for Parents and Pupils* (London, HM Government).

DH (2002) *Listening, Hearing and Responding. Department of Health Action Plan: Core Principles For the Involvement of Children and Young People* (London, Department of Health).

DH and DfES (2004) *National Service Framework for Children, Young People and Maternity Services. Core Standards. Change for Children. Every Child Matters* (London, Department of Health).

DHSS (1982) *Child Abuse. A Study of Inquiry Reports 1973–1981* (London, DHSS).

Dixon, J., Knight, T. and Tibble, M. (2003) *Feedback for the Ministerial Listening Tour, July 2003 Young People Talk, Ministers Listen. Research Report RR503* (London, DfES).

Dixon-Woods, M., Young, B. and Heney, D. (1999) Partnerships with children, *BMJ*, 319, pp. 778–780.

Duncan, N. (2003) Awkward customers? Parents and provision for special educational needs, *Disability and Society*, 18(3), pp. 341–356.

Durrant, M. (1995) *Creative Strategies for School Problems: Solutions for Psychologists and Teachers* (New York, Norton).

Dyson, A. and Robson, E. (1999) *School, Family, Community: Mapping School Inclusion in the UK* (Leicester, Youth Work Press for the Joseph Rowntree Foundation).

Dyson, A., Lin, M. and Millward, A. (1998) *Effective Communication Between Schools, LEAs and Health and Social Services in the Field of Special Educational Needs* (London, DFEE).

Dyson, A., Millward, A. and Todd, L. (2002) *A Study of 'Extended' Schools Demonstration Projects. Research Report 381* (London, DfES).

Easen, P., Ford, K., Higgins, S., Todd, L. and Wootten, M. (1996) *The Educational Achievement Strategy: An Evaluation of the First Eighteen Months of Operation of the Project in the West End of Newcastle upon Tyne* (Newcastle, Department of Education, Newcastle University).

Easen, P., Atkins, M. and Dyson, A. (2000) Inter-professional collaboration and conceptualisations of practice, *Children and Society*, 14, pp. 355–367.

Edwards, A. (2004) The new multi-agency working: collaborating to prevent the social exclusion of children and families, *Journal of Integrated Care*, 12(5).

Edwards, A. (2005) *Multi-Agency Working for the Prevention of Social Exclusion: Using Activity Theory to Understand Learning Across Organisations* (Birmingham, Birmingham University).

Edwards, R. (ed.) (2002) *Children, Home and School. Regulation, Autonomy or Regulation?* (London, RoutledgeFalmer).

Ellis, V. and High, S. (2004) Something more to tell you: gay, lesbian or bisexual young people's experiences of secondary schooling, *British Educational Research Journal*, 30(2), pp. 213–225.

Engestrom, Y. (1996) Developmental studies of work as a testbench of activity theory: The case of primary care medical practice, in: S. Chaiklin and J. Lave (eds) *Understanding Practice. Perspectives on Activity and Context* (Cambridge, Cambridge University Press).

Engestrom, Y. (1999) *The Activity System* http://www.helsinki.hi/~jengestr/activity/6b.htm.

Engestrom, Y., Miettinen, R. and Punamaki, R. (eds) (1999) *Perspectives on Activity Theory* (Cambridge, Cambridge University Press).

Evans, R. (1975) Children 'at risk': identification before school, *Aspects of Education*, 20, pp. 10–23.

Farrell, P., Harraghy, J. and Petrie, B. (1996) The statutory assessment of children with emotional and behavioural difficulties, *Educational Psychology in Practice*, 12(2), pp. 80–85.

Fielding, M. (2001) Beyond the rhetoric of student voice: new departures or new constraints in the transformation of 21st century schooling, *Forum*, 43(2), pp. 100–109.

Flutter, J. and Ruddock, J. (2004) *Consulting Pupils. What's in it for schools?* (London, RoutledgeFalmer).

Foucault, M. (1979) *Discipline and Punish: the Birth of the Prison* (Harmondsworth, Peregrine Books).

Foucault, M. (1980) *Power/Knowledge: Selected Interviews and Other Writings* (New York, Pantheon Books).

Foucault, M. (1984) *The History of Sexuality* (Harmondsworth, Peregrine Books).

Fox, M. (2004) 'But it is also soul destroying . . .' Parents views on how services can support them bringing up children in the inner city, *Educational and Child Psychology*, 21(3), pp. 6–15.

Frederickson, N., Dunsmuir, S., Lang, J. and Monsen, J. (2004) Mainstream–special school inclusion partnerships: pupil, parent and teacher perspectives, *International Journal of Inclusive Education*, 8(1), pp. 37–57.

Freeman, J., Epston, D. and Lobuvits, D. (1997) *Playful Approaches to Serious Problems* (New York, Norton).

Fundudis, T. (2003) Consent issues in medico-legal procedures: how competent are children to make their own decisions?, *Child and Adolescent Mental Health*, 8(1), pp. 18–22.

Gabe, J., Olumide, G. and Bury, M. (2004) 'It takes three to tango', a framework for understanding patient partnership in paediatric clinics, *Social Science and Medicine*, 59, pp. 1071–1079.

Galloway, D., Armstrong, D. and Tomlinson, S. (1994) *The Assessment of Special Educational Needs. Whose Problem?* (Harlow, Longman).

Gameson, J., Rhydderch, G., Ellis, D. and Carroll, T. (2005) Constructing a flexible model of integrated professional practice Part 2 – process and practice issues, *Educational and Child Psychology*, 22(4), pp. 41–55.

Garth, B. and Aroni, R. (2003) 'I value what you have to say'. Seeking the perspective of children with a disability, not just their parents, *Disability and Society*, 18(5), pp. 561–576.

Geller, G., Tamor, E.S., Bernhardt, M.S., Fraser, G. and Wissow, L.S. (2003) Informed consent for enrolling minors in genetic susceptibility research: a qualitative study of at-risk children's and parents' views about children's role in decision-making, *Journal of Adolescent Health*, 32(4), pp. 260–271.

Gersch, I., Holgate, A. and Sigston, A. (1993) Valuing the child's perspective, *Educational Psychology in Practice*, 9(1), pp. 36–45.

Gewirtz, S., Ball, S.J. and Bowe, R. (1995) *Markets, Choice and Equity in Education* (Buckingham, Open University Press).

Gibbs, S. and Stoker, R. (eds) (1996) Perspectives of children and young people, *Educational and Child Psychology*, 13(2), pp. 31–40.

Gimrax, N. and Bell, P. (2004) *CAMHS. Teeside Investing in Children. Interim Report. June 2004* (Durham, Investing in Children and Tees and North East Yorkshire NHS Trust).

Gliedman, J. and Roth, W. (1981) Parents and professionals, in: W. Swann (ed.) *The Practice of Special Education* (Oxford, Blackwell).

Goodley, D., McLaughlin, J., Clavering, E., Fisher, P., Tregaskis, S. and Salkeld, N. (2006) Enabling Practices of Care and Support for Parents with Babies with Special Care Needs. ESRC Funded Research. Executive Summary (University of Sheffield and University of Newcastle).

Greco, V. and Sloper, P. (2004) Care co-ordination and key worker schemes for disabled children: results of a UK-wide survey, *Child: Care, Health and Development*, 30, pp. 13–20.

Gregory, E. (1994) Cultural assumptions and early years' pedagogy: the effect of the home culture on minority children's interpretation of reading in school, *Language, Culture and Curriculum*, 7, pp. 111–124.

Grossman, V. (2005) An investigation into the roles children have in educational psychology practice (M.Sc. in educational psychology, dissertation, Newcastle University).

Hallett, C. (1995) *Interagency Coordination in Child Protection* (London, HMSO).

Hallett, C. and Prout, A. (eds) (2003) *Hearing the Voices of Children. Social Policy for a New Century* (London, RoutledgeFalmer).

Halliday, J. and Asthana, S. (2004) The emergent role of the link worker: a study in collaboration, *Journal of Interprofessional Care*, 18(1), pp. 17–28.

Hamill, P. and Boyd, B. (2003) Interviews with young people about behavioural support: equality, fairness and rights, in: M. Nind, K. Sheehy and K. Simmons (eds) *Inclusive Education: Learners and Learning Contexts* (London, David Fulton).

Hancock, R. and Mansfield, M. (2002) The literacy hour: a case for listening to children, *The Curriculum Journal*, 13(2), pp. 183–200.

Hannon, P. (1995) *Literacy, Home and School* (London, Falmer).

Harker, M. (2001) How to build solutions at meetings, in: Y. Amjal and I. Rees (eds) *Solutions in Schools* (London, Brief Therapy Press).

Harker, R.M., Dobel-Ober, D., Lawrence, J., Berridge, D. and Sinclair, R. (2003) Who takes care of education? Looked after children's perceptions of support for educational progress, *Child and Family Social Work*, 8, pp. 89–100.

Harris, P. (2000) Happy Families. The experiences and perceptions of lesbian mothers and their children at home and school (M.Sc. in educational psychology, dissertation, Newcastle University).

Hart, C. and Chesson, R. (1998) Children as consumers, *BMJ*, 316, pp. 1,600–1,603.

Hart, R.A. (1992) *Children's Participation: From Tokenism to Citizenship* (Florence, UNICEF).

Hart, S. (1996) *Beyond Special Needs: Enhancing Children's Learning Through Innovative Thinking* (London, Paul Chapman).

Hayes, B. (2002) Community, cohesion and inclusive education, *Educational and Child Psychology*, 19(4), pp. 75–90.

Henshaw, L. (2003) Special educational needs and the law: some practical implications, *Education and the Law*, 15(1), pp. 3–18.

HMSO (1988) *Report of the Inquiry into Child Abuse in Cleveland 1987 by Dame Butler-Sloss* (London, HMSO).

HMSO (1989) *Discipline in Schools. Report of the Committee of Enquiry Chaired by Lord Elton* (London, HMSO).

HMSO (2003) *Every Child Matters* (London, HMSO).

Hobbs, C. (2000) Initial consultation with children and young people: the practice of educational psychologists (D.Ed.Psy. assignment, Newcastle University).

Hobbs, C. (2005) Professional consultation with pupils through teaching about learning (D.Ed.Psy. dissertation, Newcastle Upon Tyne).

Hobbs, C., Taylor, J. and Todd, L. (2000) Consulting with children and young people. Enabling educational psychologists to work collaboratively with children and young people, *Educational and Child Psychology*, 17(4), pp. 107–115.

Holzman, L.H. (1996) Pragmatism and dialetical materialism in language development, in: H. Daniels (ed.) *An Introduction to Vygotsky* (London, Routledge).

Hudak, G.M. and Kihn, P. (ed.) (2001) *Labelling. Pedagogy and Politics* (London, RoutledgeFalmer).

Hughes, M. (1993) Parents' views – rhetoric and reality, in: R. Merttens, D. Mayers, A. Brown and J. Vass (eds) *Ruling the Margins: Problematising Parental Involvement* (London, IMPACT Project, University of North London).

Hughes, M., Wikeley, F. and Nash, T. (1994) *Parents and their Children's Schools* (Oxford, Blackwell).

Hughes, R. (2002) The voice of the child within the family group conferencing process (M.Sc. in educational psychology, dissertation, Newcastle University).

Hugman, R. (1991) *Power in Caring Professions* (Basingstoke, Macmillan).

James, A. and Prout, A. (1990) *Constructing and Reconstructing Childhood. Contemporary Issues in the Sociological Study of Childhood* (London, Falmer Press).

Johnson, T. (1972) *Professions and Power* (Basingstoke, Macmillan).

Kagan, C., Lawthom, R., Duckett, P. and Burton, M. (2006) Doing community psychology with disabled people, in: D. Goodley and R. Lawthom (eds) *Disability and Psychology. Critical Introductions and Reflections* (Basingstoke, Palgrave).

Kalyanpur, M., Harry, B. and Skrtic, T. (2000) Equity and advocacy expectations of culturally diverse families' participation in special education, *International Journal of Disability, Development and Education*, 47(2), pp. 119–136.

Kay, E., Tisdall, M., Kay, H., Cree, V.E. and Wallace, J. (2004) Children in need? Listening to children whose parent of carer is HIV positive, *British Journal of Social Work*, 34, pp. 1,097–1,113.

Kendrick, A. (1995) Supporting families through inter-agency work: youth strategies in Scotland., in: M. Mill, R.K. Hawthorne and D. Part (eds) *Supporting Families* (Edinburgh, HMSO).

King, E.N. and Wilson, M. (2006) Educational psychology in Scotland: More community than school based?, *Educational and Child Psychology*, 23(1), pp. 68–79.

Kirby, P. and Bryson, S. (2002) *Measuring the Magic? Evaluating and Researching Young People's Participation in Public Decision-Making* (London, Carnegie Young People Initiative).

Kirby, P., Lanyon, C., Cronin, K. and Sinclair, R. (2003a) *Handbook. Building a Culture of Participation. Involving Children and Young People in Policy, Service Planning, Delivery and Evaluation* (London, DfES).

Kirby, P., Lanyon, C., Cronin, K. and Sinclair, R. (2003b) *Research Report. Building a Culture of Participation. Involving Children and Young People in Policy, Service Planning, Delivery and Evaluation* (London, DfES).

Larson, M.S. (1977) *The Rise of Professionalism – A Sociological Analysis* (Berkeley, CA, University of California Press).

Leadbetter, J. (2004) The role of mediating artifacts in the work of educational psychologists during consultative conversations in schools, *Education Review*, 56(2), pp. 134–145.

Lightfoot, J. and Sloper, P. (2003a) Having a say in health: Involving disabled and chronically ill children and young people in health service development, *Children and Society*, 17, pp. 277–290.

Lightfoot, J. and Sloper, P. (2003b) Having a say in health: Involving young people with a chronic illness or physical disability in local health services, *Children and Society*, 17, pp. 277–290.

Lingard, C. (2002) Views and perceptions of young people in the role and practice of educational psychology (Doctorate assignment, conference presentation, Manchester University).

Lloyd, G., Stead, J. and Kendrick, A. (2001) *Hanging on in There. A Study of Inter-agency Work to Prevent School Exclusion in Three Local Authorities* (London, National Children's Bureau).

Mac an Ghaill, M. (1994) *The Making of Men: Masculinities, Sexualities and Schooling* (Buckinghamshire, Open University Press).

Macbeth, A. (1993) How can home-learning become part of our education system?, in: R. Merttens, D. Mayers, A. Brown and J. Vass (eds) *Ruling the Margins: Problematising Parental Involvement* (London, IMPACT Project, University of North London).

MacKay, T. (2006) The educational psychologist as community psychologist:

holistic child psychology across home, school and community, *Educational and Child Psychology*, 23(1), pp. 7–15.

Macrae, S. (2003) Social exclusion: exclusion from school, *International Journal of Inclusive Education*, 7(2), pp. 89–102.

Madge, N. and Fassam, M. (1982) *Ask the Children. Experiences of Physical Disability in the School Years. 'So what, I'm handicapped . . . who cares? Not me'* (London, Batsford Academic).

Marks, D., Burman, E., Burman, L. and Parker, I. (1995) Collaborative research into education case conferences, *Educational Psychology in Practice*, 11(1), pp. 41–48.

McConachie, H.R. (1999) Conceptual frameworks in evaluation of multi-disciplinary services for children with disabilities, *Child: Care, Health and Development*, 25(2), pp. 101–113.

McDermott, R.P. (1996) The acquisition of a child by a learning disability, in: S. Chaiklin and J. Lave (eds) *Understanding Practice. Perspectives on Activity and Context* (Cambridge, Cambridge University Press).

McGuiness (1998) *From Thinking Skills to Thinking Classrooms* (London, HMSO).

Merttens, R. and Vass, J. (1990) *Sharing Maths Cultures : IMPACT* (London, Falmer Press).

Merttens, R. and Vass, J. (ed.) (1993) *Partnerships in Maths: Parents and Schools* (London, Falmer Press).

Milbourne, L. (2005) Children, families and interagency work: experiences of partnership work in primary education settings, *British Education Research Journal*, 31(6), pp. 675–695.

Mittler, P. and McConachie, H. (1983) *Parents, Professionals and Mentally Handicapped People. Approaches to Partnership* (London, Croom Helm).

Mittler, P. and Mittler, H. (1982) *Partnership with Parents* (Stratford-upon-Avon, National Council for Special Education).

Monk, G., Winslade, J., Crocket, K. and Epston, D. (1996) *Narrative Therapy in Practice. The Archaology of Hope* (San Francisco, CA, Jossey-Bassey).

Mooney, A. and Blackburn, T. (2003) *Children's Views on Childcare Quality. Report No: RR482* (London, DfES).

Moran, P., Ghate, D. and van der Merwe, A.C. (2004) *What Works in Parenting Support? A Review of the International Evidence, Research Report No. 574* (London, DfES and Home Office).

Morgan, A. (1995) Taking responsibility: working with teasing and bullying in schools, *Dulwich Centre Newsletter*, 2 and 3, pp. 16–28.

Morgan, A. (1999) *Once Upon a Time . . . Narrative Therapy with Children and Their Families* (Adelaide, Dulwich Centre Publications).

Morgan, A. (2000) *What is Narrative Therapy? An Easy-to-Read Introduction* (Adelaide, Dulwich Centre Publications).

Morris, J. (1998) *Don't Leave Us Out. Involving Disabled Children and Young Children with Communication Impairments* (York, Joseph Rowntree Foundation).

Morris, J. (2002) *A Lot to Say. A Guide for Social Workers, Personal Advisors and Others Working With Disabled Children and Young People With Communication Impairments* (London, Scope).

Munro, E. (2001) Empowering looked-after children, *Child and Family Social Work*, (6), pp. 129–137.

Murray, P. and Penman, J. (eds) (1996) *Let Our Children Be. A Collection of Stories* (Sheffield, ibk initiatives).

Neighbourhood Renewal Unit (2006) *Young People and Regeneration: Case Studies* (London, ODCPM Publications).

Newson, E. (1976) Parents as a resource in diagnosis and assessment, *Early Management of Handicapping Disorders, Review of Research and Practice*, 19.

ODPM (Office of the Deputy Prime Minister) (2004) Tackling social exclusion: taking stock and looking to the future: emerging findings (London, ODPM).

Ofsted (2003) *Inspecting Schools. Framework for Inspecting Schools. Effective from September 2003* (London, Ofsted).

O'Neill, M. and Stockell, M. (2003) A narrative perspective. Introduction to narrative ideas and practices (Workshop notes, Newcastle University, July 2003).

Owen, R., Hayett, L. and Roulstone, S. (2004) Children's views of speech and language therapy in school: consulting children with communication difficulties, *Child Language Teaching and Therapy*, 20(1), pp. 55–73.

Parker, I. (1999) Deconstructing psychotherapy, in: I. Parker (ed.) *Deconstructing Psychotherapy* (London, Sage).

Partlett, M. (1991) The assessment of hearing-impaired children, in: D. Schon (ed.) *The Reflective Turn. Case Studies in and On Educational Practice* (New York, Teachers College Press).

Perkin, H. (1996) *The Third Revolution. Professional Elites in the Modern World* (London, Routledge).

Perkins, H. (1989) *The Rise of Professional Society. England since 1880* (London, Routledge).

Phillips, J. (2003) Deconstructing 'Sean'. The language of prejudice for a child looked after by the local authority, *Educational and Child Psychology*, 20(1), pp. 64–75.

Prout, A. (2005) *The Future of Childhood* (Abingdon, Routledge).

Pugh, G. (1989) Parents and professionals in pre-school services: is partnership possible?, in: S. Wolfendale (ed.) *Parental Involvement. Developing Networks Between School, Home and the Community* (London, Cassell).

Punch, S. (2002) Interviewing strategies with young people: the 'secret box', stimulus material and task-based activities, *Children and Society*, 16, pp. 45–56.

Quinton, D. (2004) *Supporting Parents. Messages from Research* (London, Jessica Kingsley Publishers).

Read, J.M. (1985) *A Critical Appraisal of the Concept of Partnership* (Department of Applied Social Studies, University of Warwick).

Reay, D. (1996) Contextualising choice: social power and parental involvement, *British Educational Research Journal*, 22(5), pp. 581–596.

Rhodes, J. and Ajmal, Y. (1995) *Solution Focused Thinking in Schools* (London, BT Press).

Richardson, R., Wood, A. and Lawrence, D. (1999) *Inclusive Schools, Inclusive Society. Racism and Identity on the Agenda* (Stoke-on-Trent, Trentham Books).

Riddell, S., Brown, S. and Duffield, J. (1994) Parental power and special educational needs: the case of specific learning difficulties, *British Educational Research Journal*, 20(3), pp. 327–344.

Roaf, C. (2002) *Co-ordinating Services for Included Children. Joined-Up Action* (Buckingham, Open University Press).

Roaf, C. and Lloyd, C. (1995) *Multi-Agency Work with Young People in Difficulty* (York, Joseph Rowntree Foundation).

Roffey, S. (2004) The home-school interface for behaviour: A conceptual framework for co-constructing reality, *Educational and Child Psychology*, 21(4), pp. 95–109.

Roose, G.A. and John, A.M. (2003) A focus group investigation into young children's understanding of mental health and thei views onappropriate services for their age group, *Child: Care, Health and Development*, 29(6), pp. 545–550.

Rudduck, J. and Chaplain, R. (1995) *School Improvement. What Can Pupils Tell Us?* (London, David Fulton).

Rudduck, J. and Flutter, J. (2000) Pupil participation and pupil perspective: 'carving a new order of experience', *Cambridge Journal of Education*, 30(1), pp. 75–89.

Ruegger, M. (2001) Seen and heard but how well informed? Children's perceptions of the Guardian ad Litem service, *Children and Society*, 15, pp. 133–145.

Russell, S. and Carey, M. (eds) (2004) *Narrative Therapy. Responding to Your Questions* (Adelaide, Dulwich Centre Publications).

Sammons, P., Power, S., Elliot, K., Robertson, P., Campbell, C. and Whitty, G. (2003) *Key Findings from the National Evaluation of the New Community Schools Pilot Programme in Scotland* (London, Institute of Education, University of London).

Sandbaek, M. (1999) Children with problems: focusing on everyday life, *Children and Society*, 13, pp. 106–118.

Sandow, S., Stafford, D. and Stafford, P. (1987) *An Agreed Understanding? Parent–Professional Communication and the 1981 Education Act* (Windsor, NFER-Nelson).

Scottish Executive (2001) *For Scotland's Children. Better Integrated Children's Services* (Edinburgh, Scottish Executive).

Scottish Executive (2003) *A Partnership for a Better Scotland* (Edinburgh, Scottish Executive).

Seaman, P. and Sweeting, H. (2004) Assisting young people's access to social capital in contemporary families: a qualitative study, *Journal of Youth Studies*, 7(2), pp. 173–190.

Shemmings, D. (2000) Professionals' attitudes to children's participation in decision-making: dichotomous accounts and doctrinal contests, *Child and Family Social Work*, 5, pp. 235–243.

Shier, H. (2001) Pathways to participation: openings, opportunities and obligations. A new model for enhancing children's participation in decision-making, in line with Article 12.1 of the United Nations Convention on the Rights of the Child, *Children and Society*, 15, pp. 107–117.

Simkins, E.A. (2001) An exploration into providing written feedback for children: an educational psychologist's perspective (M.Sc. in educational psychology dissertation, Newcastle University).

Simmons, J. (2003) A study investigating GP views on child participation in their medical consultations and whether there is a difference when allowing child participation in medical consultations for physical compared with mental illness (B.Sc. psychology unpublished project, Newcastle University).

Skrtic, T.M. (1995) Deconstructing/reconstructing the professions, in: T.M. Skrtic (ed.) *Disability and Democracy: Reconstructing (Special) Education for Postmodernity* (New York, Teachers College Press).

Slee, R. (1996) Disability, class and poverty: School structures and policing identities, in: C. Christensen and F. Rizvi (eds) *Disability and the Dilemmas of Education and Justice* (Buckingham, Open University Press).

Sloper, P. (1999) Models of service support for parents of disabled children. What do we know? What do we need to know?, *Child: Care, Health and Development*, 25(2), pp. 85–99.

Sloper, P. and Lightfoot, J. (2002) Involving disabled and chronically ill children and young people in health service development, *Child: Care, Health and Development*, 29(1), pp. 15–20.

Smith, C. and Nylund, D. (eds) (1997) *Narrative Therapies with Children and Adolescents* (London, The Guilford Press).

Stafford, A., Laybourn, A. and Hill, M. (2003) 'Having a say': Children and young people talk about consultation, *Children and Society*, 17, pp. 361–373.

Statham, D. (2000) Guest editorial: partnership between health and social care, *Health and Social Care in the Community*, 8(2), pp. 87–89.

Stead, J., Lloyd, G. and Kendrick, A. (2004) Participation or practice innovation: tensions in inter-agency working to address disciplinary exclusion from school, *Children and Society*, 18, pp. 42–52.

Swain, J. and Walker, C. (2003) Parent-professional power relations: parent and professional perspectives, *Disability and Society*, 18(5), pp. 547–560.

Tates, K. and Meeuwesen, L. (2001) Doctor–patient–child communication. A (re)view of the literature, *Social Science and Medicine*, 52, pp. 839–851.

Thomas, D. (1978) *The Social Psychology of Childhood Disability* (London, Methuen).

Thomas, G. and Loxley, A. (2001) *Deconstructing Special Education and Constructing Inclusion* (Buckingham, Open University Press).

Thomas, N. and O'Kane, C. (1999) Children's participation in reviews and planning meetings when they are 'looked after' in middle childhood, *Child and Family Social Work*, 4, pp. 221–230.

Thorpe, L. (2003) I want someone to listen to me: consultation with children in special circumstances. Unpublished paper to inform the development of the NSF for children and young people (London, NSPCC).

Tiplady, L. (2005) What evidence is there that school-based services of counselling in two Full Service Extended Schools are meeting pupils' needs and views? (Diploma in psychology, unpublished report, Newcastle University).

Tisdall, K., Wallace, J. and Bell, A. (2005) *Seamless Services: Smoother Lives. Assessing the Impact of Local Preventative Services on Children and Their Families. Children in Scotland* (York, Joseph Rowntree Foundation).

Tizard, B. and Hughes, M. (1984) *Young Children's Learning* (London, Fontana).

Todd, E.S. (2000a) The problematic of partnership in the assessment of special educational needs (Ph.D. thesis, Newcastle University).

Todd, E.S. and Higgins, S. (1998) Power in professional and parent partnerships, *British Journal of Sociology of Education*, 19(2), pp. 227–236.

Todd, L. (2000b) Letting the voice of the child challenge the narrative of professional practice, *Dulwich Centre Journal*, 1 and 2, pp. 73–79.

Todd, L. (2003a) Disability and the restructuring of welfare: the problem of partnership with parents, *International Journal of Inclusive Education*, 7(3), pp. 281–296.

Todd, L. (2003b) The views of the child: enabling pupil participation, *Special Children*, 154, pp. 22–25.

Todd, L. (2003c) The views of the child: setting learning targets, *Special Children*, 155, pp. 16–20.

Todd, L. (2006) Enabling practice for professionals: the need for practical post-structuralist theory, in: R. Lawthom (ed.) *Disability and Psychology. Critical Introductions and Reflections* (Basingstoke, Palgrave).

Tolley, E., Girma, M., Stanton-Wharmby, A., Spate, A. and Milburn, J. (1998) *Young Opinions Great Ideas* (London, National Children's Bureau).

Tomlinson, S. (1981) *Educational Subnormality: A Study in Decision Making* (London, Routledge and Kegan Paul).

Tomlinson, S. (1982) *A Sociology of Special Education* (London, Routledge and Kegan Paul).

Topping, K. (1986) *Parents as Educators: Training Parents to Teach Their Children* (London, Croom Helm).

Topping, K. (1995) *Paired Reading, Spelling, and Writing: The Handbook for Parent and Peer Tutoring in Literacy* (New York, Cassell).

Topping, K. (1996) Reaching where adults cannot. Peer education and peer counselling, *Educational Psychology in Practice*, 11(4), pp. 23–29.

Topping, K. and Wolfendale, S. (eds) (1985) *Parental Involvement in Children's Reading* (London, Croom Helm).

Townsley, R., Abbott, D. and Watson, D. (2004) *Making a Difference? Exploring the Impact of Multi-Agency Working on Disabled Children with Complex Health Care Needs, Their Families and the Professionals who Support Them* (Bristol, The Policy Press).

Troman, C. and Sangster, A. (2003) NSF Agenda Day. Report 2003 (Durham, Investing in Children).

Vernon, S., Lundblad, B. and Hellstrom, A.L. (2003) Children's experiences of school toilets present a risk to their physical and psychological health, *Child: Care, Health and Development*, 29(1), pp. 47–53.

Vincent, C. (2000) *Including Parents? Education, Citizenship and Parental Agency* (Buckingham, Open University Press).

Vincent, C. and Martin, J. (2000) School-based parents' groups – a politics of voice and representation, *Journal of Educational Policy*, 15(5), pp. 459–480.

Vincent, C. and Warren, S. (1997) A 'different kind' of professional? Case studies of the work of parent-centred organisations, *International Journal of Inclusive Education*, 1(2), pp. 143–161.

Walker Perry, N. and Wrightsman, L.S. (1991) *The Child Witness: Legal Issues and Dilemmas* (London, Sage).

Wardekker, W.L. and Miedema, S. (2001) Identity, cultural change and religious education, *British Journal of Religious Education*, 23(2), pp. 76–87.

Warnock, M. (1978) *Report of the Committee of Enquiry into the Education of Handicapped Children and Young People* (London, HMSO).

Watson, N., Shakespeare, T., Cunningham-Burley, S., Barnes, C., Corker, M., Davis, J. and Priestly, M. (1999) *Life as a Disabled Child: A Qualitative Study of Young People's Experiences and Perspectives*. ESRC Research Programme. Children 5–16: Growing into the Twenty-First Century. Grant number L129251047 (Swindon, ESRC Report).

Webster, A. and Hoyle, E. (2000) The 'new professionalism' and the future of educational psychology, *Educational and Child Psychology*, 17(2), pp. 93–104.

Weingarten, K. (1994) *The Mother's Voice. Strengthening Intimacy in Families* (New York, Guilford Press).

White, J.A. and Wehlage, G. (1995) Community collaboration: if it is such a good idea, why is it so hard to do?, *Educational Evaluation and Police Analysis*, 17(1), pp. 23–38.

White, M. (2003) Narrative practice and community assignments, *The International Journal of Narrative Therapy and Community Work*, 2, pp. 17–55.

White, M. (2004) *Narrative Practice and Exotic Lives: Resurrecting Diversity in Everyday Life* (Adelaide, Dulwich Centre Publications).

White, M. and Epston, D. (1990) *Narrative Means to Therapeutic Ends* (London, W.W. Norton).

Wigfall, V. and Moss, P. (2001) *More than the Sum of its Parts? A Study of a Multi-Agency Child Care Network?* (London, National Children's Bureau).

Williams, S. (1993) *Evaluating the Effects of Philosophical Enquiry in a Secondary School* (Derby, Village Community School).

Wilson, B. and Wyn, J. (1993) Educational inequality and cultural conflict, in: L. Angus (ed.) *Education, Inequality and Social Identity* (London, Falmer).

Winslade, J. and Monk, G. (1999) *Narrative Counselling in Schools* (Thousand Oaks, CA, Corwin Press).

Wise, S. (2000) *Listen to Me! The Voices of Pupils with Emotional and Behavioural Difficulties* (Bristol, Lucky Duck).

Wolfendale, S. (1983) *Parental Participation in Children's Development and Education* (London, Gordon and Breach Science Publishers).

Wolfendale, S. (1985) Overview of parental participation in children's education, in: K. Topping and S. Wolfendale (eds) *Parental Involvement in Children's Reading* (London, Croom Helm).

Wolfendale, S. (1989) Parental involvement and power-sharing in special needs, in: S. Wolfendale (ed.) *Parental Involvement. Developing Networks between school, home and the community* (London, Cassell).

Wolfendale, S. (1992a) *Empowering Parents and Teachers : Working for Children* (London, Cassell).

Wolfendale, S. (1992b) *Primary Schools and Special Needs 2e: Policy, Planning and Provision* (London, Cassell).

Wolfendale, S. (1993) Parent's contribution to assessing, recording and communicating their children's development and progress: review and prospects, in: R. Merttens, D. Mayers, A. Brown and J. Vass (eds) *Ruling the Margins: Problematising Parental Involvement* (London, IMPACT Project, University of North London).

Wolfendale, S. (1995) The Code of Practice and parents: a stimulus for reappraisal of EPs' work with parents, *Educational and Child Psychology*, 12(3), pp. 73–79.

Wolfendale, S. (1997a) Delivering services for children with special needs: the place of children, in: S. Wolfendale (ed.) *Working with Parents or SEN Children After the Code of Practice* (London, David Fulton).

Wolfendale, S. (ed.) (1997b) *Meeting Special Needs in the Early Years. Directions in Policy and Practice* (London, David Fulton).

Wolfendale, S. (ed.) (1997c) *Working with Parents or SEN Children After the Code of Practice* (London, David Fulton).

Wolfendale, S. and Bastiani, J. (eds) (2000) *The Contribution of Parents to School Effectiveness* (London, David Fulton).

Wolfendale, S. and Cook, G. (1997) *Evaluation of Special Educational Needs Parent Partnership Schemes* (London, DFEE).

Wolfendale, S. and Einzig, H. (eds) (1999) *Parenting Education and Support* (London, David Fulton).

Wolfendale, S. and Topping, K. (eds) (1996) *Family Involvement in Literacy. Effective Partnerships in Education* (London, Cassell).

Woodhead, M. (1991) Psychology and the cultural construction of 'children's needs', in: M. Woodhead, P. Light and R. Carr (eds) *Growing up in a Changing Society* (London, Routledge, Open Universiy).

Woolfson, R.C. and Harker, M. (2002) Consulting with children and young people: young people's views of a psychological service, *Educational and Child Psychology*, 19(4), pp. 35–46.

Wyness, M.G. (2000) *Contesting Childhood* (London, Falmer).

Wyse, D. (2001) Felt tip pens and school councils: children's participation rights in four English schools, *Children and Society*, 15, pp. 209–218.

Young, B., Dixon-Woods, M., Windridge, K.C. and Heney, D. (2006) Managing communication with young people who have a potentially life threatening chronic illness: qualitative study of patients and parents, *BMJ*, 326, pp. 305–309.

Index

Note, *t* denotes a table; *f* a figure